A Kid's Guide to Plants of the Great Lakes Region

A Kid's Guide to Plants of the Great Lakes Region

Including Southern Ontario with Cool Facts, Activities and Recipes

Written and Illustrated by

Philippa Joly

with contributions from Danielle Hagel

HARBOUR PUBLISHING

Table of Contents

Author's Note   vi

Safety First!   vii

Introduction   1

1 Indigenous Peoples of the Great Lakes Region   6

2 Regions and Plants Covered by This Book   9

3 Plant Names and Language   12

4 Dos and Don'ts of Wildcrafting Plants   14

5 Understanding Plant Families   17

6 Poisonous Plants 21

7 Invasive Plants 28

8 Plant Profiles 35
Spring 36
Summer 97
Autumn 142
Winter 162

9 For Parents and Educators 190

Glossary 202
Acknowledgements 208
Selected References 210
Index 211
Image Credits 214
About the Author 215

Author's Note

This book was written on the K'ómoks, Pentlatch, Qualicum, Homalco, Klahoose, Tla'amin, We Wai Kai and We Wai Kum lands where I live. It was dreamed up on the Lekwungen, W̱SÁNEĆ, Musqueam, Squamish and Tsleil-waututh lands where I have lived in the past. I am indebted to all the **Indigenous** knowledge keepers who have taught me what I know about plants directly and indirectly. Thank you to the Indigenous Nations of the Great Lakes Region for sharing their home with settlers and for carefully tending the plants of this place. I hold in my heart the complex historical and ongoing displacement of Indigenous people from their lands, and the destruction of the land, as I work with the plants of these lands. I thank, also, my own ancestors for carrying the knowledge they have through many eras of their own displacement. This book is dedicated to the plants themselves. May they always be wild and free.

Safety First!

This book contains information about plants you can eat and plants you cannot eat. There are some very poisonous plants in this area. It's very important that anyone using this book and eating wild plants be sure of what they're eating. Before you eat a plant in the wild, ask a knowledgeable adult if it's okay to do so. There are also activities in this book that must be done with the help of an adult so as to keep you safe. The author and the publisher are not at fault in the unlikely chance you get hurt by eating wild plants or doing an activity with them. Stay curious and stay safe.

Caution! Spotted Water Hemlock is in the carrot family but it is also one of the most poisonous plants found in the Great Lakes region.

Yellow Dock or *Rumex crispus*

Introduction

What's So Cool About Plants Anyway?

People often ask me how I first got interested in plants. I tell them about my older sister. I always thought she was pretty cool, and I wanted to be like her. One day, when she was about sixteen and I was fourteen, she came back from a trip she went on with a friend to some little island where there was no electricity or paved roads. I was jealous. I wanted to go too, but I was too young. I asked what she did there, and she said she had taken a class about plants with a woman who was named something like River or Waterfall or Ocean. "Look," my sister said, pointing at a little plant at our feet. "That one is called Yellow Dock or *Rumex crispus*. You can eat it." In that moment, a light went on inside me. There was something captivating about those words: *Rumex crispus*. They sounded like magic. I repeated those words, *Rumex crispus*, to myself over and over as I delved into my fascination with plants that has now lasted over twenty-eight years. And I still look up to my big sister, even if I am half an inch taller than she is.

You may not have a big sister or ever have heard such weird-sounding words as *Rumex crispus*, but you probably

Learn New Words

. . . .

When words are in **this font** it means they're in the Glossary on page 202. Look there to learn the meaning of words you don't know!

have your own story about plants. No matter who you are or where you live, plants are a big part of our lives. Plants are the food we eat. Bread is made from wheat, which is a grass. Cotton is grown to spin into fabric to make clothing. Paper we use at school is made from trees. Some fuel we put in our cars is made from corn. Much of our medicine is or was once made from plants. We play on grass lawns and twirl "helicopter seeds" dropped from trees. These are all ways we have relationships with plants. Can you imagine a world without them?!

Plants are everywhere. If you live in a city, Dandelions pushing up through the cracks in the sidewalk remind us of the strength of one little seed. Weeds like Wild Carrot and Thistle have long roots that help break up hard, compacted earth. Trees line the streets, there are roses in your neighbour's garden, and your grandma might grow peas on her little balcony. For those of you who don't live in the city, there are so many plants that you may not even notice them. They may just blur into a wall of green.

In our world today, kids spend a lot of time inside on screens or in scheduled activities. Many kids don't know the names of the plants around them. Maybe you can win at a video game, but would you know what to eat in the woods? Learning about plants might seem like a waste of time when you have homework to do or a text to send. But with an uncertain future due to climate change and a natural world that needs caring for, knowing about plants can change and maybe even save your life.

2   Introduction

If you are hungry, it would be good to know which plants you can eat and which are poisonous. And have you ever had a lonely, terrible day when you felt like you had no one to talk to? Plants are always there to listen. Plants offer medicine, sustenance, building materials and even replacements for toilet paper!

Plants want to be known. For as long as there have been humans, we have had relationships with plants. Find your favourite abandoned lot, community garden, **old-growth forest**, creekside, park or backyard and start there. Choose a plant or two and find out who they are, what they might be good for, what makes them special. Just like you and me, every plant is unique and has something to offer. The more we know about plants, the more we care about them. This care then leads us to caring for the places these plants live.

One of the reasons I love my work is because I get to spend so much time outside around plants. I run a nature school where kids get to have fun interacting with plants and the land around them. We get to do things like eat wild foods, walk across logs over creeks, learn to identify bird calls, practice our animal tracking skills, find animal kill sites and learn to feel more at home in the outdoors. There are nature schools in many cities and towns all over Turtle Island (what is now called North America). If you are interested in going to one, just look online for "nature schools where I live."

I also work as an herbalist, which means I harvest wild plants, make them into medicine and then help people who

> At nature school, we nibble the fresh leaves of Garlic Mustard, we make crowns out of Willow and we get so muddy tracking racoons that one kid said, "I'm so dirty, my mom is going to kill me! This is awesome!"

> How many pop songs do you know all the words to? Now, how many bird songs do you know?

are sick get better using the healing powers of plants. Just like in the old days, before there were doctors and drug companies, there were people who knew which plant to give someone for a cold, which plant will stop bleeding and which plant will help with aches and pains. Plants are very generous; they don't ask for money. The only thing they ask is that we keep where they live healthy and treat them with respect. We can all relate to that!

This book is written in the hope that you will learn to love plants and the places where they grow. There are lots of ideas for games and activities that you can do with the plants, so that you are not just learning their names, but also forming relationships with them. You can share this book with the adults in your life and you may need an adult's help to do some of the activities. If your adults are interested in learning more about plants, there's a section just for them at the back of the book.

I wrote this book from my perspective, which is the only perspective I know. I grew up in Victoria, British Columbia, Canada, on Songhees/Lekwagan territory, where I learned to love the plants of that area. My skin is white, and my ancestors are from France and Scotland. Although I know a lot about plants, I will never know as much as someone whose family has been on this land since time immemorial (that means longer than anyone can remember). I am honoured to have learned about plants from people who have spent time with Indigenous Elders and then shared that information with me. I have tried to make my sharing about

4   Introduction

plants as respectful as possible. I have spent a lot of happy times in the Great Lakes region, but it's not my home, nor do I know all about the plants here. So I teamed up with my friend, Danielle Hagel, to write this book. She is a kids' nature educator and an herbalist as well as an artist and naturalist who lives in Guelph, Ontario. Danielle knows and loves the plants of the Great Lakes region, and now she gets to share that with you!

Now, go outside and say hi to the first plant you see. It's waiting to tell you all about itself. Then see if you can find it in this book. See you outside!

Taya gathers buttercups by the river.

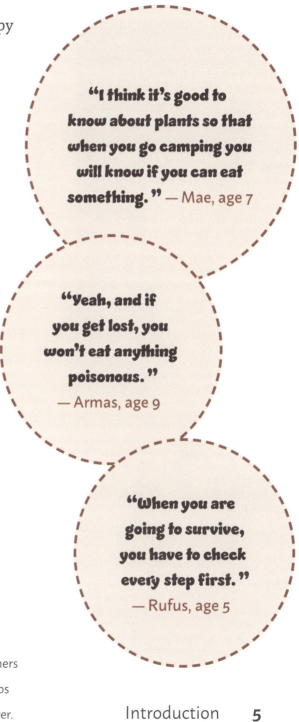

"I think it's good to know about plants so that when you go camping you will know if you can eat something." — Mae, age 7

"Yeah, and if you get lost, you won't eat anything poisonous." — Armas, age 9

"When you are going to survive, you have to check every step first." — Rufus, age 5

Introduction   5

1

Indigenous Peoples of the Great Lakes Region

Indigenous People have been living in the Great Lakes region since time immemorial. This is a vast and varied region, and the people who lived here and continue to live here are also varied, from the Dene Cree people of the north to the Osage people in the south. One thing that ties all these peoples together is their connection to the land and the plants and animals who live on it.

Before the first Europeans came, all of Turtle Island (North America) was a complex and densely populated world of people living their lives in myriad ways, from huge city states, to rich coastal fishing cultures, to desert-living people with ingenious ways of moving water, to people living in polar lands with ice and snow. North America was anything but an empty land with a few nomadic bands of hunting and gathering people moving haphazardly across it!

When the first Europeans came to the Great Lakes region in the mid-1500s, they saw village after village surrounded by miles of agriculture growing corn, beans and squash, known as the Three Sisters. They also saw rich land they wanted and people they wanted to take for slaves. Missionaries came to force people to become Catholic. Fur traders came to hunt animals, especially beavers, for their pelts to be made into fancy hats for people in Europe. With them they brought guns, alcohol, germs and ways of being never before experienced by the people of this region.

In some places, almost all of the Indigenous people were killed so that the settlers could steal their food and land. In other places, they were forced off their land and made to move far away from their homes. In every place, Indigenous people did what they could to resist the violence of the European settlers, to maintain their cultures and to keep their families safe. Although much was lost in this attempted **genocide**, there are nearly a million Indigenous people living and practicing their cultures in the Great Lakes region today.

When we read about Indigenous people in books, it's often in the past tense: "people *relied* on Cattail for many important parts of their culture." Instead, we should say "people *rely* on Cattail for many important parts of their culture." Indigenous people are not just in the past, and many of them still rely on plants and trees in their cultures today. There are Great Lakes Indigenous people who are helping to connect Indigenous and non-Indigenous people to the wonderful and generous world of plants. Even though much of the land has been changed, covered up by cities, flooded

Look who's hiding in the Three Sisters!

The other Taya shows us an Osage Orange.

by dams or turned into **monoculture** farms, there are still many places that Indigenous people have been tending forever. People continue to harvest wild rice along lake edges despite the pressure of private property in cottage country. They continue to hunt and trap and fish. They tend Maple trees to gather syrup and they tend the beautiful gardens that grow their life-giving plants of corn, beans and squash.

An important part of working with plants is forming a relationship with the land where you live. Learning whose traditional territory you live on, or what Indigenous nation lives where you live, is one step toward honouring the people whose land you are on and their ancestors who tended it. Much of what we know about the uses of plants in the Great Lakes region has come to us from the Indigenous Elders of this place. This is important to remember for two reasons. Firstly, recognizing who our teachers are, even if we are learning about the plants through books, helps keep alive respect for the traditions and the cultures that support them. Secondly, because we live and learn on land that has been tended and shaped by thousands of years of Indigenous culture, even if those cultures are not visible to us now, we are always on Indigenous land. To find out whose land you live on, use this digital map: native-land.ca.

2

Regions and Plants Covered by This Book

The Great Lakes region is made up of the biggest **watershed** in North America. This region spans an enormous area starting at the Hudson's Bay in the north and going all the way southwest to the Mississippi River. To the west, it touches the Ohio Valley and to the east it goes all the way to the Atlantic Ocean in New York. The five Great Lakes that give this region its name are Lake Superior, Lake Erie, Lake Ontario, Lake Michigan and Lake Huron. These are bordered by the Canadian province of Ontario and the eight US states of Illinois, Indiana, Michigan, Minnesota, New York, Ohio, Pennsylvania and Wisconsin. There are many big cities in this region, and yet, there are also many wild places as well. If you live in any of these places—whether city or country—you will find some of the plants in this book.

The Great Lakes are the biggest concentration of **freshwater** in the world! They contain 21 per cent of all the world's non-ocean water. Because of this, the lakes and the rivers

A boggy guild of Fir, Aspen and Blueberry.

that flow in and out of them are very important **habitats** to the animals, plants and humans who depend on them. As cities were built along the edges of the lakes, factories were built as well. Soon large ships came to bring in materials and ship out manufactured goods. Some of these factories and ships dumped toxic chemicals and pollutants into the water, which caused many fish and bird populations to decline or even face near extinction. This pollution also made it unsafe

Just watching the river flow.

for people to eat the fish or to harvest wild plants in the area. In the last 20 years, a lot of effort has been made to limit the use of toxic chemicals and to clean up the lakes.

This region is made up of a mix of rich, moist soils and bedrock. To the north are forests of Spruce and Fir, and rolling through the whole area are woodlands of Maple, Ash, Hickory, Oak, Beech, Birch and Aspen. The cold winters and hot, humid summers give us the distinct seasons we associate with the **northern hemisphere**. The temperature changes make the **deciduous** leaves turn bright colours in the fall and allow the sap to flow in the Maples in early spring, when the trees can be tapped to make syrup. Plants grow quickly throughout the spring and summer as they soak up the summer rainstorms and turn heat and sunshine into food. This region is great for growing and gathering wild foods!

3

Plant Names and Language

You will notice as you read this book that when we talk about plants we use different types of names. Common names are the names English-speaking people have given to the plants. Every plant (and animal for that matter) in the region already had an Indigenous name when the Europeans came along and "discovered" and renamed them. There are many Indigenous languages spoken throughout this region such as Algonquian and Iroquoian. In these languages, not only do plants have names, sometimes there are also names for each part of the plant, or for how a plant is used or eaten. I am not including the Indigenous names in this book,

Black-Eyed Susan.

because they're not mine to share, nor do I know many of them. It would take an encyclopedia to list them all!

Many common names of plants are descriptive, like Blue Violet or Black-Eyed Susan. Some plants have been given more than one common name, like Queen Anne's Lace, which is also called Wild Carrot. This can be confusing. Sometimes more than one plant has the same name, like the Fir trees, one of which is a "true" Fir and one which is not. This is one of the reasons **botanists** use Latin names when talking about plants. Every plant has only one Latin name, so we can't mix them up. Latin is considered a "dead" language, meaning no country or culture speaks it, and only scholars and scientists use it. So they chose to use Latin names as an overall naming or classification system.

Usually, when people write about plants, the plant name is spelled with a lowercase letter, like "dandelion." I have chosen to use uppercase letters when writing about plants, as in "Dandelion." When we spell our names or the names of places, they start with capitals. By capitalizing the plant's name, I am hoping to remind you to see them not as "things" but as living individuals who are in a relationship with the world around them and who deserve respect.

Chapter 3

Dos and Don'ts of Wildcrafting Plants

Plants and people have a long history together. Humans have always harvested plants to use for food, medicine, tools, clothing or other purposes. Today, we call this **wildcrafting**. When we harvest plants with awareness, they will continue to flourish in the future. Although plants can be abundant, we have to keep in mind that we are sharing them with the rest of our community: the animals and insects that rely on them for food or shelter, the **ecosystem** that depends on them in many invisible ways, or the other people who may want to harvest them as well. People are supposed to interact with plants. Do gently pick a leaf of Mint and eat it. Don't grab all the leaves off the Milkweed as you walk by. Treat plants with respect and they will be there for you.

Wildcrafting means gathering plants with care.

Here are some tips to help you become an **ethical** harvester:

Get to know the area where you are harvesting.
- Whose traditional territory are you on?
- How many plants are there?
- Do any animals use these plants for food?
- Does anyone else harvest plants from this place?
- Do dogs do their business on these plants? Yuck!
- Is there nearby traffic or businesses that might be polluting the area?
- How do the place and its plants change with the seasons?

Leave rare plants alone.
Never pick rare plants. If you are unsure, don't pick it and check local conservation guidelines.

Don't take more than one plant out of ten.
A general rule with common plants is not to take more than one plant out of ten. Observe approximately how many plants are in the patch, and for every ten plants, just pick one plant.

Be careful with roots.
If you are harvesting roots, remember that unless the plant can regenerate by replanting a part of the root, you are killing the whole plant by taking the root.

Chapter 4   15

Symbols Used in this Book

Edible

Not edible but won't kill you

Rare, so don't pick it!

This plant has medicinal uses.

This activity needs an adult's help.

Poisonous, don't touch it!

Think about the flowers' future.
Harvesting flowers means harvesting the future fruit of the plant. Roses turn to rose hips, for example. **Pollinators** like bees, butterflies and hummingbirds need flowers for food.

Leave some seeds behind.
If you are picking a plant when it's in seed, make sure to leave some seeds scattered in the area for regeneration.

Check in with the plants.
Return to your harvest spots in every season so you can see the impact on the plants and their ecosystems. Some plants may like to be thinned out, allowing more light in or allowing room for the patch to spread out.

Watch out for poison.
Never harvest plants near roads, under power lines or other places **herbicides** or **pesticides** are sprayed.

Leave no trace.
Fill in holes, re-cover roots and replace leaves or mulch. This assures the place can recover easily and that the remaining plants will continue growing.

Thank the plants.
Some people like to say thank you, sing a song while they harvest or leave a token of thanks. If you do this, make sure it's **compostable** and small.

5

Understanding Plant Families

Like people, plants have families. Every plant belongs to a family. Each family of plants has certain characteristics. For example, just like people in your family may have brown hair, plants in the Mint family have square stems. Learning about plant families can help us learn how to quickly identify plants and some of their uses.

Plant Families

Here are five common plant families to get to know.

Carrot (Apiaceae or Umbelliferae)

Although there are many edible plants in this family, like Carrots, Parsley and Cumin, some of the most poisonous plants in the world are in this family as well, so please do not gather these plants without a knowledgeable adult's help! The poisonous plants are Water Hemlock, Poison Hemlock and Giant Hogweed. Common and not-so-poisonous plants

in the Carrot family include Wild Carrot or Queen Anne's lace, Sweet Cicely and Angelica.

Flowers in the Carrot family are white, yellow or reddish brown. Their seeds are small clusters forming large **umbels**, like umbrellas, that usually have a strong smell when crushed. The stems are often hairy and hollow with long and feathery leaves.

Lily (Lilaceae)

Some of the region's most beautiful wild flowers are in the Lily family, like Trout Lily, Trilliums and Wild Leeks. There are a lot of showy garden flowers in this family, and even Asparagus and Onions are Lilies! When you think of Lilies, you can think in threes. There are three petals, three **sepals**, six **stamens**, and the seed capsule has three chambers to it. The leaves of plants in the Lily family all have **parallel veins**, meaning they run side by side.

Mint (Mentha)

Many common kitchen herbs are in the Mint family, including Oregano, Rosemary, Thyme and Mint, of course. Some of the many wild plants in the Mint family are Motherwort, Bee Balm, Mad Dog Skullcap and Field Mint.

The small flowers in the Mint family are white, pink, purple or blue and are shaped like little trumpets. The stems are square with **lance-shaped** leaves that grow **opposite** each other on the stem. All these plants smell strongly, but not always "minty." They contain high amounts of **volatile oils**, which give them their scent and also mean that many of them are good for colds and flus.

Rose (Roseacea)

Most Rose family plants make edible fruits, like Blackberries, Raspberries, Apples, Crab Apples, Pears, Strawberries and Hawthorn.

These sweet-smelling flowers are pink, white, yellow or red, and always with petals in multiples of five. The stems are often thorny or hairy. The leaves in the Rose family are usually opposite, lance-shaped and **serrated**.

Sunflower or Aster (Asteraceae or Compositae)

Some common wild plants in the Aster family are Yarrow, Chicory, Tansy, Hairy Cat's Ear, New England Aster, Goldenrod and, of course, Dandelion! Lettuce is in the

Mae and the Mint.

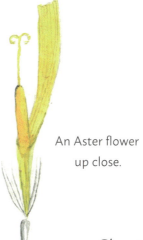

An Aster flower up close.

Chapter 5

A summer field of Chicory.

Chicory.

Aster family too. The flowers in the Aster family are tricky! These yellow, orange, white, purple or pink flowers look like one big flower, but when you look closer, there are many, sometimes hundreds of tiny flowers all bunched together. Some Aster flowers have outer **bracts** that look like petals but are really a kind of leaf. The rest of the "real" leaves are often hairy or soft and lance-shaped. The Aster family is the second-largest family of plants in the world after orchids.

A **subclass** of the Aster family is the Dandelion family. These flowers are usually yellow to orange and have straight-ended petals. The leaves on these plants are often toothed, hairy or serrated. The plants in the Dandelion subfamily are edible, but all have milky white sap in the stems that makes them bitter.

6

Poisonous Plants

Getting to know plants is exciting! All of a sudden there are friends, snacks, medicines or crafts all around you. But getting to know plants really well is important because there are some very poisonous ones that grow in this region and many have look-alikes that can be hard to tell apart without practice.

Some important things to keep in mind when meeting any plant for the first time, and especially poisonous ones, is to consult an adult who knows about plants before you touch them. Only eat plants you have eaten before with an adult. If you need to handle a poisonous plant for further identification, wear gloves and make sure to wash your hands well afterwards. Do not put your hands on your face or in your mouth. Most poisonous plants will make you sicker the more you eat. If you eat one little tiny crumb of Water Hemlock, it can give you a tummy ache, but if you eat a whole bulb, you can get terribly sick and vomit and have fevers. If you eat a whole root, you can die. You don't

> Never touch or eat a plant if you don't know what it is.

> "Vein to the cut, hurts my gut!"

Spotted Water Hemlock: look but don't touch.

> The great Greek philosopher Socrates died from drinking Water Hemlock tea.

want any of these things to happen, so be careful but curious when meeting poisonous plants.

One of the most poisonous plants we live near is called **Spotted Water Hemlock** (*Cicuta maculata*). This is in the Carrot or Apiaceae family. You will find them in wet, mucky areas, like the banks of the Eramosa River in southwestern Ontario, and growing in the cool shade of Cedar trees, beside Blue Lobelia and Bottle Gentian. Learning how to tell these plants apart from other plants in the Carrot family is important because there are many other wonderful plants in the Carrot family to get to know, like Wild Carrot (*Daucus carota*) and Sweet Cicely (*Osmorhiza claytonii*).

Up close with the Spotted Water Hemlock.

A great way to identify Spotted Water Hemlock is by looking closely at the leaves. The **veins** of these leaves go to the cut in the leaf, whereas other plants in the Carrot family have leaves with the vein going to the tip of the leaf. Another way to tell this plant apart from its non-poisonous cousins is by cutting open the base of the stalk while wearing gloves. The bulging part at the base is made up of hollow chambers. One of these is enough to kill a cow! It causes **convulsions** and shuts down the **nervous system**. Holy cow!

Here are some other poisonous plants to keep an eye out for. Spotted Water Hemlock and other members of the Carrot family are sometimes mistaken for **Giant Hogweed** (*Heracleum mantegazzianum*). But Giant Hogweed, as its

Chapter 6 23

How can we love poisonous plants even though they can hurt us? This question requires a bit of thought. Take Water Hemlock, for example. Despite its notoriety as the most poisonous plant in North America, Water Hemlock is easy to love. It's very beautiful, with dark-purple stems, lacy white flowers and deeply toothed leaves. Poisonous plants like Water Hemlock remind us humans that not everything in nature is for us to eat or use. They remind us to slow down, to be mindful of our surroundings and aware of what we touch and pick so we don't accidentally hurt ourselves. They teach us awareness—and even reverence.

This really IS Giant Hogweed.

24   Chapter 6

name suggests, tends to tower over its look-alikes. It can grow up to 5.5 metres (18 feet) tall. Just imagine three tall people standing on each other's shoulders—that's the size of a full-grown Giant Hogweed plant! Its white flowers grow in umbels that can stretch over a metre (3 feet) wide, like poisonous patio umbrellas. Its jagged leaves look like that of parsnip. They're found along roads, ditches and streams and in wooded areas. The sap and small hairs on the stem of this plant cause itching, rashes, burns and even blisters. If you get the sap on your skin, wash the area with soap and water and avoid exposing it to the sun, which activates the rash-making chemicals in the sap.

When most people think of poisonous plants, they think of **Poison Ivy** (*Toxicodendron radicans*). These shiny, dark green leaves come in sets of three. Poison Ivy likes to grow

> Leaves of Three, Let it Be.

Notice the shiny "leaves of three" of the Poison Ivy.

Chapter 6

along forest edges, in meadows, forest openings and trails. The resins from the leaves contain an oily substance called urushiol that can give you a very painful rash. These resins can also get on shoes and animal fur and then get on your skin when you touch them. If you think you have been in contact with Poison Ivy, wash the area with warm, soapy water and launder any clothes that have touched the plant in hot water.

In the same family as Poison Ivy is **Poison Sumac** (*Toxicodendron vernix*), a small shrub or tree that grows in marshes and along pond shorelines. The dark-green oval leaves have smooth edges and sharply pointed tips. They grow alternately in groups of seven to thirteen per stem. In

Poison Sumac looks similar to Poison Ivy but is not shiny.

fall, you can spot Poison Sumac by the cream-coloured berries that droop down in long, loose clusters. All parts of the plant contain urushiol and can cause a painful, itchy rash. If you come into contact with this plant, follow the same steps as you would for Poison Ivy. Like many toxic plants, Poison Sumac isn't all bad: Its berries feed many animals, including Bobwhites, Pheasants and Grouse and contain sap that has been used to make varnish for furniture.

Pokeweed (*Phytolacca americana*) looks delicious with its dangling clusters of juicy dark-purple berries growing on hot-pink stems. But eating any part of the plant can harm humans, dogs and the livestock who nibble it along fences or in pastures. Burning in the mouth, vomiting, diarrhea or convulsions can send people to the emergency room. You can even die if you eat a lot of it. And yet, this plant is native to eastern North America and has also been known to feed birds (including Mockingbirds, Northern Cardinals and Mourning Doves), bears and even humans who have boiled the young, vitamin-rich shoots repeatedly (tossing out the water in between boils) to remove the toxins before eating them like spinach. *Phytolacca*, from Pokeweed's Latin name, means "red dye plant," and the deep-purple juice of its berries has been used to tint fabrics.

These Pokeweed berries look like candy, but will make you sick if you eat them.

Chapter 6   **27**

7

Invasive Plants

You may have heard the term **invasive plants** or **non-native** plants before. These terms refer to plants that do not originate in North America. Unlike **native plants**, which have evolved in intricate relationships with the soil, insects and other plants and trees, non-native plants don't have natural competition, predators and diseases here to keep them in check. Without these things, they can take over an ecosystem. They may grow faster and bigger than the native plants present and be very good at taking up space in the soil. In these ways, non-native plants can disrupt plant communities and throw ecosystems out of balance.

Still, many of the common plants we know in this part of the world are non-native plants. Plants strive to rebalance what is off. Most grasses we see here are non-native. Many plants that grow where the soil or **ecology** has been **disturbed** or clear cut are non-native, and they hold together soil that might otherwise erode. In an ideal situation, humans would not be clear-cutting forests, nor would they have brought these seeds in, and the plants would not be

Garlic Mustard is a tasty snack—add it to your spring salad.

Like most things in the world, deciding whether these plants are "good" or "bad" can be difficult. Here are some questions that may guide you:
- What is the invasive plant doing?
- Is it providing food for birds?
- Is it shading out wildflowers?
- Is it holding in soil?
- Is it causing animals to get sick?
- Are the roots pushing out other roots?

destroying fragile ecosystems. Here are some common non-native plants in the Great Lakes region.

Garlic Mustard (*Alliaria petiolata*) is named after its scent. If you scrunch its leaves in your hand, you'll be greeted with a strong garlicky smell. This edible leafy green likely arrived in New York State about 150 years ago. It was brought by European settlers who used it as food and medicine because it's rich in vitamins A and C. It has since become prolific in forests all over North America. In addition to leaking chemicals into the soil that make it hard for other plants to grow, Garlic Mustard displaces spring flowers like

Chapter 7

> Plants aren't bad. It's not the Garlic Mustard's fault that it's very good at surviving and thriving.

Trillium and is toxic to butterfly larvae and **fungi** that help trees grow.

One yummy way to keep these leafy greens in check? Eat them! With a mild garlic flavour and bitter bite, they're perfect in salad or blended into pesto. You can also go online to find an annual Garlic Mustard pull in your community. In May, groups gather to round up the plants before they take hold in local conservation areas and parks for the summer.

Buckthorn (*Rhamnus cathartica*), which is native to Europe and western Asia, is another plant that has a terrible reputation. It's a small tree that has shiny, grey bark and spikes on the twigs. Buckthorn's leaf veins meet at the very tip of their small, glossy leaves. It grows quickly, outcompeting other plants for space and sunlight. Buckthorn is happy to grow in poor, disturbed or unhealthy soil, where, like Garlic Mustard, its roots give off chemicals that make it difficult for other plants to grow. Those roots are tough and will sprout new shoots even if the trunks are cut down. This is one stubborn, well-adapted plant!

And that's not all. Buckthorn berries and bark are **emetic** and **laxative**, meaning they can irritate your stomach, causing you to throw up or have diarrhea if you accidentally eat them. Not fun! For all of these reasons, Buckthorn inspires anger and even fear in well-meaning nature lovers who see only its potential to cause harm. But it's important to remember that plants themselves are not inherently bad.

Buckthorn.

Chapter 7

Try This!

MAKE YOUR OWN BUCKTHORN INK

Gather Buckthorn berries when they turn deep-purple in the fall. In a small pot, add one part Buckthorn berries to two parts water. Bring water to a boil and let it simmer for half an hour or more to extract the colour. Strain out the berries and let the liquid simmer again until it's reduced by about half or until it's concentrated to your liking. At this stage, the ink will be a purple colour that transforms to green as it dries. You can create a brighter shade of green by adding a teaspoon of alum (potassium aluminum sulphate, which is available at bulk foods stores for use in canning). Try using it with a natural paint brush or carve the end of a twig into a point to use as your drawing tool. Buckthorn ink keeps in a jar in the fridge for several weeks. Caution: Label the jar clearly so nobody mistakes the ink for jam or syrup!

Supplies needed:
- a couple of handfuls of Buckthorn berries
- small pot
- strainer
- jar with tight-fitting lid

Common Buckthorn berries.

Sap Green

This is the colour Buckthorn berries make.

31

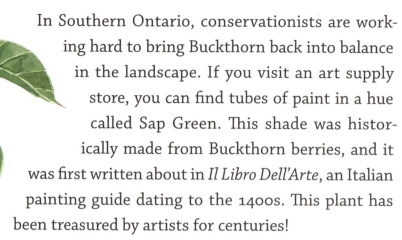
Japanese Knotweed.

In Southern Ontario, conservationists are working hard to bring Buckthorn back into balance in the landscape. If you visit an art supply store, you can find tubes of paint in a hue called Sap Green. This shade was historically made from Buckthorn berries, and it was first written about in *Il Libro Dell'Arte*, an Italian painting guide dating to the 1400s. This plant has been treasured by artists for centuries!

Japanese Knotweed (*Reynoutria japonica*) is originally from Asia and is considered one of the most invasive plant **species** worldwide. It's sometimes mistaken for Bamboo, with hollow stems and **nodes** along its stalk like Bamboo. But unlike Bamboo's long, narrow leaves, Japanese Knotweed leaves are red when they're young, then become green and heart-shaped with the edges curling up.

This plant has superpowers! And, like most superpowers, it can be used for good or for evil. It's able to grow up to 8 centimetres (3 inches) a day, so you can almost see it grow in front of your eyes. In fact, this plant can survive almost anywhere—through drought and temperatures as low as -35°C (-31°F). It sprouts roots 3 metres (10 feet) deep and is so strong it can crack pavement apart! Japanese Knotweed lives in dense thickets that can fill in waterways, fields, abandoned lots and even take over buildings.

Good thing Japanese Knotweed has good superpowers too! It flowers in late summer or early autumn, which is great for bees because they bloom when many other plants are

This is what Japanese Knotweed looks like when it is young.

not flowering anymore. Beekeepers in the eastern United States make honey from Japanese Knotweed, and it's edible. Like its cousin Rhubarb, it has a tangy lemony flavour. The young shoots can be peeled and eaten raw or prepared as you would Rhubarb.

The other cool thing about Japanese Knotweed is that medicine made from the root is helpful in treating Lyme's Disease, which is passed along through tick bites. And, in a surprising coincidence, Japanese Knotweed is spreading to the very same places as the tick that carries Lyme's Disease.

Some other common invasive and non-native plants are Thistle, which brings up nutrients from the soil but is prickly and takes over grazing pastures; Yellow Iris, which absorbs heavy metals in wastewater ponds but can squeeze out fish and bird habitats; and St. John's Wort, which dominates pastures and can poison cows and sheep who graze on it, but helps humans who use it as a treatment for mild depression. When we know the land and the plants, we then

Our job as people who care for the land and know about plants is to notice how a plant is affecting where it grows.

Try This!

CAN'T BEAT ME!

Do you think you are strong enough to outsmart Japanese Knotweed? If it grows where you live, you can experiment with ways to stop it. What happens if you cover it with dirt, put concrete blocks on top of it, shade it with a tarp, dig it out or pen it in with goats or pigs so they eat it? How long does it take to grow again after you have tried to get rid of it? Some people have dug down 3 metres (10 feet) to try to dig out the roots. The next year, the plant grew back twice as big! If you can find a way to get rid of Japanese Knotweed without using harmful chemicals, you could be a millionaire!

have an idea of how and when to help. You might see some Buckthorn or Garlic Mustard just beginning to take hold in your favourite woods and pull it out. But the big thicket of Blackberry might be pruned and enjoyed for the berries it feeds you and your family throughout the winter. Using these plants for food, medicine and crafts are great ways to make friends with them.

8

Plant Profiles

Here are some plants you may be likely to meet in wild areas, parks, cities and forests in the Great Lakes region. They're arranged by season so you will know when to look for them. Within each season they're arranged alphabetically. The Latin name is in *italics* next to each common name. You'll also find some great activities to do with the plants in every season. There are many ways to learn about plants. Use all your senses: your eyes, your hands, your ears, your nose and your mouth!

Sophia and Margret play the blindfold game.

Spring

In spring, plants begin their growth. It's a time of fresh new shoots, blossoms, flowers and edible greens. Bees are busy **pollinating** flowers. The soil is warming up enough for seeds dropped last fall to begin to sprout.

Cottonwoods in fluff.

American Basswood

Tilia americana

Description

A common tree of woodlands, riverbanks and meadows, American Basswood can be identified by its asymmetrical heart-shaped leaves. The bark of young trees is smooth and grey and becomes rougher and more furrowed with age. You can find young Basswood stumps with multiple shoots that have been cut down by beavers, who love the soft wood. The fragrant, light-yellow flowers bloom in summer and make a delicious tea or infused honey.

Cool Facts about American Basswood

Spoon carver John Wager of the Curve Lake Anishinaabe First Nation uses strips of the inner bark of Basswood to weave bags, among many other things. Basswood inner bark can be stripped from a felled tree and soaked in a pond for several months. This process is called retting, and it's a step in processing many plant fibres. This results in a strong, waxy, sweet-smelling fibre that can be used to make cordage rope.

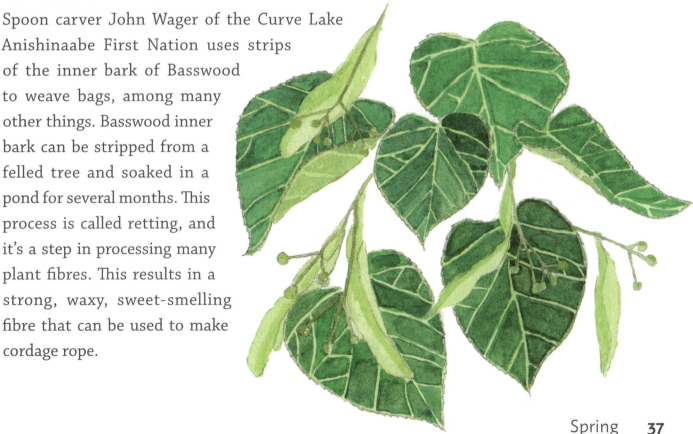

Spring

The careful harvest of drying Basswood flowers for a calming tea.

Harvesting Tip

Basswood leaves are edible anytime but are tastiest when they're young and just starting to open. They should be glossy, smooth and about the size of a toonie. Mature Basswood leaves can be blanched and stuffed with grains and vegetables, as you would grape leaves.

American Basswood

Try This!

MEET A TREE

Supplies needed:
- trees
- bandana
- a partner

This group activity is great for getting to know trees—and our many senses—in a deep way. Get into pairs. One person is blindfolded and their partner's job is to walk them carefully, but not in a straight line, to a tree. There, the blindfolded person "meets" the tree, using all their senses except sight. They can feel the bark, the branches and the shape of the leaves. Have them smell the sap or the buds and taste the needles or the fruits. Have them listen to the tree itself and the birds in its branches. Now lead the blindfolded person back a different way to the starting point. Remove their blindfold and ask them to find their tree! This is also a great time to have the participants draw their tree, developing their sense of sight. This tree will probably make an impression on the person and be remembered for a long time.

Milliano "meets" a tree.

American Basswood

Blue Violet

Viola odorata

Description

All Violets have flat flowers with five petals. Of the many species of Violet in the Northeast, the non-native Blue Violet stands out for its smooth, heart-shaped leaves and strongly scented, deep-purple-blue flowers. This abundant edible spring flower is easy to find growing on front lawns, fields, and any other green space you can think of.

Cool Facts about Violets

The lower petal of Violet flowers has stripes on it that act like a landing pad for bumblebees and butterflies, encouraging them to collect nectar. The flower is designed so that when the bees land, they knock against the pollen and then carry the pollen to the next flower they visit, thus making sure the flowers get pollinated.

Blue Violets have a lovely flavour and scent that has been used for centuries in cooking and perfumery; there is a reason their scientific name contains the word "*odorata*," meaning "fragrant." When someone pops a Violet in their mouth for the first time, the reaction is always the same: "Wow, that's really good!"

Try This!

MAKE YOUR OWN VIOLET SYRUP

Violet syrup is as easy to make as it is magical to taste. Place 125 grams (1 cup) of freshly picked Blue Violets in a jar and cover them with 250 millilitres (1 cup) of boiling water. Let the Violets infuse in the water for a few hours or overnight. Place the Violet infusion in a saucepan over low heat, then add 250 millilitres (1 cup) of sugar or honey and stir until dissolved. Remove the syrup from the heat, let it cool and strain it through cheesecloth or a mesh strainer to remove the spent flowers. Pour the cooled syrup into a jar. Add it to soda water, drizzle it over pancakes or fruit salad, mix it into cake frosting for a purple hue, or use it for whatever sounds yummy to you. This syrup can be stored in the fridge for up to three months.

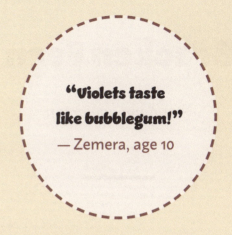

"Violets taste like bubblegum!"
— Zemera, age 10

Supplies needed:
- Blue Violets
- small jar
- saucepan
- sugar or honey
- cheesecloth or mesh strainer

Nibble This!

All species of Violet in the Northeast are edible, though it's best not to eat rare ones.

Delicate but yummy Blue Violets.

Blue Violet

Bracken Fern

Pteridium aquilinum

Description

Bracken Fern can grow as tall as me! (But I'm only 5′3″.) With big feathery **fronds** that are divided into leaves on either side of the stem, this Fern looks different from the other common Ferns in the region. It likes to grow in open clearings, meadows, on roadsides and in other sunny locations.

Cool Facts about Bracken Fern

Bracken Fern is a fast-growing **deciduous** Fern. It dies back in the winter and in the spring unfurls from little green spirals. It grows so fast that from one day to the next, you can almost see it unfurling. Bracken Fern is one of the most common Ferns in the world, growing all across the northern hemisphere.

> "Dried Bracken Fern makes a good bed when you lay them down on the ground. I like to build a nest out of them and have a nap." — Briar, age 8

Spring

Try This!

MEASURE A FERN

Supplies needed:
- notebook
- pencil
- measuring tape

Watching plants grow sounds like a boring thing to do. But not always. When you can almost see the plant grow before your eyes, you can see the magic of **photosynthesis**, or how plants "eat." In April or May, find a patch of Bracken Fern that you can visit every day, or every week. Bring a tape measure, pencil and notebook. Choose one Bracken Fern that is just coming up and measure it. Make a drawing in your notebook and record your observations. Continue to measure it regularly, drawing it as it changes, and noting how quickly it grows. Here are some questions to ask: Does it grow at the same rate throughout the spring? Are there times it grows faster or slower? What helps it to grow so quickly? How long does it take to reach full size? How tall would you be if you grew this fast?

Breah and Alexander measure Bracken Fern.

Bracken Fern

Cattail

Typha latifolia

Description

Have you ever seen a hot dog growing on a stick in the shallow water of ponds, marshes, lakesides and ditches? Well, then you have seen Cattail. It's a tall plant, up to 2.5 metres (9 feet) tall, with long, narrow, flat, kind of spongy leaves that grow almost straight up. In the spring, Cattail sends up shoots that then turn into a dense cluster of tiny brown flowers that form that hot dog shape. Above the brown part is a spike of light-brown pollen. Late in the summer, when Cattail goes to seed, the "hot dog" turns into white fluff that goes sailing across the water.

Cool Facts about Cattail

What plant can be a lantern, diapers, pancakes, corn on the cob, food, a roof, a sleeping mat, medicine, a duck, clothes, ropes, dishes, pillows and a blanket?! Cattail! In her book *Braiding*

Sweetgrass, Robin Wall-Kimmerer calls Cattail the "Walmart of the marsh," or just "Wal-marsh," because of how many ways it can be used. The stalks can be cut at the bottom with a flowering top, and this "hot dog" can be dipped in oil to make a lantern or torch. The seed fluff was and can be used to stuff pillows, mattresses, and diapers. A flour can be made from the pollen and turned into pancakes. When the seed heads are first coming out and are green, they can be steamed and eaten like corn on the cob. The roots and young shoots can be harvested, peeled and eaten. Mats, hats, capes, blankets, dishes and roof tiles can all be made by weaving Cattail leaves. The goo from the stem is very soothing when applied to sunburns and rashes. Rope and twine can be made from the fibre of the leaves and stalks. And finally, a duck that floats can be made by folding Cattail leaves together. All these uses for Cattail were like Walmart for people before the days of stores.

CAUTION: When harvesting the roots and shoots, be sure not to confuse Cattail with Yellow Iris, which is poisonous and a spreading invasive plant around lakes and marshes.

Cattail 45

Quack quack! A Cattail duck sets sail.

Try This!

CATTAIL DUCKS

Cut a long Cattail leaf at its base. Starting from the cut end of the leaf, fold the leaf around itself in sections as long as your hand; this forms the base of the duck. Leave enough of the end of the leaf to be folded up to become the duck's neck, then fold the tip of the leaf over to make the beak. You can tie the body of the duck together with a thin strip torn from another leaf of Cattail. Now try to float your duck on the water. You may have to adjust its balance if it tips over.

Nibble This!

Harvesting Cattail is a fun and messy job, best done on a warm day with your pants rolled up or even in a bathing suit! The roots and shoots of Cattail are quite good to eat. Cattail spreads by **rhizomes**, which are roots that run along the surface of the ground. In spring and then again in fall, these roots have shoots on them that can be snapped off, peeled and eaten raw or cooked. Be certain that you are harvesting Cattail and not Iris, which is poisonous and looks similar when they're leafing out. The inner white part of the fleshy rhizomes can be eaten the same way. To harvest the pollen to use as a protein-rich flour, place a paper bag over top of the pollen stem and shake the bag, releasing the pollen.

The kids at Salix School liked the shoots of the Cattail so much they began fighting over them. It's best to harvest with calm gratitude, otherwise you might end up covered from head to toe in mud!

Harvesting Cattail shoots.

Zemera eats the Cattail shoot.

Chickweed

Stellaria media

Miner's Lettuce

Claytonia perfoliate

Description

Chickweed is a small, spreading, low-growing plant with green heart-shaped leaves. In early summer, it grows white flowers. Miner's Lettuce is also a small, low-growing plant that clumps rather than spreads. The spade-shaped leaves are larger than Chickweed and fleshier. When the plant gets older, the leaves form a circle around the stalk, which sends up a little star-shaped flower.

Both these plants like to grow where there is some moisture in the ground, at the base of Oak trees, in lush garden beds and at the edges of woods.

Cool Facts about Chickweed and Miner's Lettuce

Both of these plants are edible and delicious early in the spring. They're yummy eaten as a snack when you're out and about, or picked to make an early spring salad. I have picked them when just enough snow has melted, and the sun comes out to warm the soil.

Because both of these plants have lots of water in them, they're soothing when applied to burns and sunburns, rashes like eczema, and Nettle stings. Just chew them up and put them on the place that hurts.

When these plants go to flower, they start to get too strong to eat and can cause an uncomfortable feeling in the back of your throat. One day in late spring, Rueben, age 9, saw a lush patch of Miner's Lettuce, grabbed a whole handful, pulled them out by the roots and gobbled them up. "Yuck!" he shouted as he spat them out. "They make my throat feel like it's full of nails." This was a little reminder from the plants to harvest them with care.

Chickweed (top) and Miner's Lettuce (left) have cute little white flowers but taste better before they bloom.

Chickweed

Nibble This!

EARLY WILD SALAD

Supplies needed:
- wild greens
- bowl
- scissors

Head out into the wild grocery store to see what you can make into a salad. April and May are great times to find all kinds of wild greens to eat. Try Chickweed, Miner's Lettuce, Dandelion greens, Dandelion flowers, Young Basswood leaves, Maple blossoms, Sheep Sorrel leaves, Spruce tips, young Curly Dock leaves or a few Trout Lily leaves. What could be better than a salad you harvest yourself from the generous free grocery store of the outdoors?! Just make sure you pick these plants gently and away from where dogs pee or cars drive.

Collecting a wild salad of Miner's Lettuce and Chickweed.

Description

Coltsfoot is so named because it was thought that the leaves look like the shape of a horse's foot. But when it comes up in the early spring, it's the flowers that come up first, before the leaves. The flowers almost look like a bunch of Dandelions, but look closely and you will see there are no leaves yet, just thick, hairy stems. Coltsfoot will be going to seed before the Dandelions are even flowering. This is when the leaves begin to appear through the mud, where Coltsfoot likes to grow, and then unfurl into their distinctive hoof shape.

Cool Facts about Coltsfoot

Because Coltsfoot flowers so early, sometimes even pushing up through late snow, it's a very important plant for bees. The first brave bees are awoken by warming days and need pollen that Coltsfoot can offer when not many other plants are flowering.

Coltsfoot's Latin name *Tussillago* comes from the word *tussis*, which means "to cough." The medicine of Coltsfoot has a long history of use for coughs, colds and flus. There was once even a candy made from the syrup of the roots.

Coltsfoot

Tussilago farfara

It's easy to see how Coltsfoot flowers could be confused for Dandelion flowers—they are both early-blooming, bright yellow flowers.

Spring 51

Dandelion

Traxacum officinale

Description

Dandelion is in the Aster family. Although many people think they know a Dandelion when they see one, this plant has many look-alikes, because the Aster family is so big. Coltsfoot looks a lot like Dandelion. Learning to tell the two apart is important, because one is good to eat and the other...not so good! (Plus, you can impress people by telling them apart!)

Cool Facts about Dandelion

Dandelions are originally from Europe and were first brought to North America as a food plant. The leaves are edible and are best eaten when they're young, in the spring before they flower. You can just pick them and munch them as a snack or add them to salads. The flowers are also edible and look pretty sprinkled in a salad.

Dandelions are very good for you as well, full of iron, potassium, calcium, and vitamins A, B, C and E. You could just eat some Dandelion leaves instead of taking your vitamins. Some people find Dandelion bitter, but this bitter quality is actually part of the medicine, helping your body clean the blood by supporting your liver. The white sap in the stem of Dandelion makes warts go away if you put it on the wart three times a day.

Spring

Dandelion gets its name from the French *dent-de-lion*, meaning "tooth of the lion," due to the sharp teeth of the leaves. It's also known as *pis-en-lit* in French, which means "to pee the bed," because Dandelion leaves can make you pee if you eat a lot.

Dandelion seeds can travel up to 100 kilometres (62 miles) on the wind. Be careful when making a wish on Dandelion seeds. The seeds can blow into your eyes and they're hard to get out!

Try This!

BRAVE BEES

Bundle up and be brave with the bees. Choose a warm, sunny day in early spring to go for a walk. Can you find any flowers? If you were a bee or another **pollinator** who needed pollen or nectar to live, could you find any today? Make a note of the temperature, the weather, and if there is any wind. If you don't see any flowers, wait a week, then try again. Which are the first flowers to come out in your area? Once you do see flowers, watch for the first pollinators. Who are they? What temperature is it when they finally come out? Where do they go when they're not visiting flowers?

Dandelion   53

Try This!

MAKE YOUR OWN KIDS' COFFEE

Supplies needed:
- Dandelion roots
- small shovel or garden trowel
- baking sheet
- kitchen knife
- coffee grinder
- oven
- cream and honey (optional)

Making Dandelion coffee.

Isabella drinks her Dandelion coffee.

Have you ever tried a sip of an adult's coffee? Did you like it? If so, now you can make your own, without all the caffeine! Lots of people don't know how great Dandelions are and wish they wouldn't grow in their lawn or garden. You can offer a Dandelion root-weeding service. Use an old butter knife or hand trowel to dig up the roots. When you have at least a handful of roots, wash them, then chop them up small (if you need help with a knife, ask an adult). Spread the roots out on a baking sheet and roast them in the oven at 350°F for about twenty minutes. Have an adult help you with the hot oven and pan. Once the roots are roasted and cooled, you can grind them up in a coffee grinder. To make the "coffee," boil 250 millilitres (1 cup) of water and simmer 1 heaping teaspoon of the roots for ten minutes. Strain and add cream and honey to taste. Yum, your very own "coffee!"

Gosling Rescue Mission

In the spring, when the beautiful lilies are flowering and the days get sunny, my family and I like to go exploring along the shorelines of lakes. Here, smooth green snakes slide from grasses, and birds' nests hide among the Cattails.

One day, we were exploring when a Canada Goose started to hiss and honk at us. He seemed like he was telling us to stay away, so we stopped where we were and watched. There, on the top of a boulder, was a mother goose sitting on her nest. We could just see her long black neck above the top of the rock. As we watched, the mother goose began to usher her goslings out of their nest. One by one, she used her black beak to force the fluffy babies to the edge of the rock and then...down the goslings fell until the father goose met them at the bottom. One, two, three, six goslings were pushed from their nests and dropped to the ground with only their little wing stubs to help break their fall. When they were all assembled at the bottom, down flew the mother goose who led the way to the lake's edge.

We were witnessing the goslings' first trip into the water! The goose family waddled along, mother in front, a string of super-fluffy cute babies trailing behind, with their father taking up the rear. Just then, we heard the high trill of a Bald Eagle. Yikes! A gosling would make a perfect afternoon snack for this Eagle. Quickly as they could, the parents began leading the goslings to the safety of the water. But on their way, a rock blocked their path. Five of the goslings figured out how to go over it, but the last and smallest gosling got stuck. Perhaps panicked by

A Canada Goose family.

the Eagle's call, the father hurried on, leaving behind the slowest sixth gosling, and soon the family started swimming away. "Peep peep peep!" cried the gosling.

Watching this, our hearts went out to the little fluff ball. Twelve-year-old Akai couldn't stand it. He tiptoed over and, gently as he could, scooped up the baby goose and carried it to the water's edge. There, it took its first paddle and was joined by happy, soft honking from its family.

Description

Cottonwood is most easily known by the sweet smell the buds give off in the spring. These buds are full of sticky golden sap. Cottonwood is a deciduous tree with waxy, heart-shaped leaves and big fluffy white **catkins** that give the tree its name. It likes to grow in moist areas, like marsh and lake edges and near streams and rivers. This tree can grow as tall as a ten-storey building, and when it gets old, the grey bark gets deeply grooved. Cottonwood is in the same family as Willow.

Eastern Cottonwood

or Necklace Poplar
Populus deltoides

Cool Facts about Cottonwood

Cottonwood is an important **wildlife tree**, which means a tree where animals like to live. When these trees get old, the bark can peel away from the trunk, making great homes for bats. The limbs blow off easily, and the resulting holes can become homes for many animals, including Pileated Woodpeckers, Northern Flickers, Chickadees, Barn Owls, Eastern Screech Owls, Golden Eyes, Buffleheads, Wood Ducks and even Black Bears and Flying Squirrels. Ospreys,

Spring 57

Great Blue Herons and Bald Eagles will often build their nests in the tops of tall Cottonwoods, giving them a great view of the waters around them for fishing. In June, when the catkins open, Cottonwood fluff floats on the breeze, sometimes making small drifts of sweet-smelling Cottonwood "snow" on the ground.

Cottonwood bud.

I once saw a family of Raccoons living in the hole of a Cottonwood, the babies sticking their cute noses out, waiting for their mother to return. They were so cute I wanted to pick one up and cuddle it. But I didn't, of course. It's important not to touch wild animals.

Harvesting Tip

It's common for branches to blow down off the Cottonwood in the big winds of winter. The easiest way to harvest the buds is from these limbs on the ground.

58   Eastern Cottonwood

Try This!

MAKE YOUR OWN COTTONWOOD BUD OIL

Cottonwood buds might be one of the best smells on earth. In the late winter and early spring, when the buds are full of sap, I often walk around with a yellow sticky nose from smelling the sap. I promise it's not snot! It's the sap from the Cottonwood. But there are more graceful ways to smell like Cottonwood. One way is to make an oil from the buds. All you need to do is bring a bag or a jar to the Cottonwood and collect the buds by breaking them off and putting them in your bag or jar. When you get home, cover the buds with an oil of your choice: olive oil, almond oil, grapeseed oil or apricot kernel oil all work well. Cover the jar with its lid and let the buds sit in this oil for about six weeks. After that, strain off the oil and compost the buds. You can wear the oil like perfume or make a healing and beautiful-smelling salve with it by following the directions for Plantain (page 115).

Supplies needed:
- Cottonwood buds
- oil like olive, avocado, apricot kernel or grapeseed
- large glass jar
- small jars or tins to put the salve in
- rubbing alcohol for cleaning up

Note: The sap is very sticky, and you will need to use rubbing alcohol to clean anything that gets sappy.

Preparing Cottonwood buds to make oil.

Eastern Cottonwood 59

Hawthorn

Crataegus spp.

Description

Hawthorn is a small deciduous tree with scaly bark that likes to grow in clearings, at roadsides and in hedgerows. It is in the Rose family, and its leaves are small and **lobed** and can resemble the leaves of Crab Apple. When the Hawthorn flowers in May, it is a wonderful cloud of small white blooms with pink-and-yellow centres that smell sweet and attract many bees. Like plants in the Rose family, there are five petals on each flower and five seeds in each berry. In late summer, the tree produces scarlet berries that ripen in the fall. Some, but not all, Hawthorn trees have long, pointy thorns.

Cool Facts about Hawthorn

There are 280 different species of Hawthorn in the world. In Europe, it's sometimes called the May Tree for the time of year it blooms. Hawthorn has long been thought of as a faerie tree, and it was said that a twig from a Hawthorn above the door would keep bad faeries away. Hawthorn makes a strong medicine for the heart, and some people believe it helps heal broken hearts. This may be true for humans, but you will be unlucky if you are a small bird, dragonfly or mouse caught by a bird called a Northern Shrike. This bird uses the thorns of the Hawthorn to impale its prey before it eats it! The dense wood of the Hawthorn is useful for making tools, and the berries can be eaten but are not delicious.

Try This!

SITTING WITH HAWTHORN

Some people, including me, believe plants can "talk." If we agree plants are alive, then surely we must be able to communicate with them somehow. In Indigenous cultures all over the world, people have learned, and continue to learn, about the uses of plants from the plants themselves. Now it's your turn.

Choose a tree that you like. There doesn't have to be any reason you like it; you can just feel drawn to it. Now, without any distractions—no books or pen, no screen or friends to talk to—find a place to sit near the tree (without getting thorns in your pants). Sit quietly for a while. Trees are like old people and they can take a while to say what they're thinking. You can introduce yourself, you can ask a question, either out loud or in your head. Pay attention to how your body feels. How does your breath feel? Do any pictures come to your mind?

It's okay if you don't have any special experience,

Akai sits with a Hawthorn tree.

> *"Wow, I had no idea it would feel so good to just sit quietly under a tree in the rain without my cell phone!"*
> — Akai, age 13

Hawthorn **61**

Do you have a favourite tree?

but you might notice you feel more at ease, more calm and happy. This is an especially great thing to do if you are feeling sad or lonely, and it can be done with any plant or tree anytime, anywhere. The more you do it, the better you get at trusting what the plant is telling you and at being quiet and still. When I first started sitting with plants, I felt like a weirdo. When I was fifteen, there was a great big Oak tree in the park next door. After especially terrible days at school, I would go and sit at the base of the Oak tree and tell it all my problems. I always felt better after. Who needs those mean kids at school anyway!?

Horsetail

Equisetum arvense

Description

Horsetail grows in two ways. The **sterile** plant does not make **spores** to reproduce. It is green, with the fringe of what looks like needles growing outward from the segments of the hollow stalk. When the plant is young, the needles are folded inward, and as it grows, they open downward. The other growth is the **fertile** plant, which makes spores for reproduction. It is creamy whitish-brown, with no needles, but a funny cone shape on top. Both these versions of Horsetail grow in spreading clumps separate from each other in rich, wet marshy ground.

Cool Facts about Horsetail

Horsetail plants are one of the oldest plants in the world! They were on earth 100 million years ago (a mind-boggling number), when the first animals crawled out of the sea. Horsetails at this time were as tall as an old-growth Fir tree! Somehow these plants survived the great extinction at the end of the Paleozoic period, when 95 per cent of life on the planet was wiped out. Well, they're not nearly as tall now, but they're still pretty amazing plants. They're actually more like Ferns

Spring

Newly sprouted Horsetail.

in that they reproduce by sending out spores instead of using seeds like other plants.

Another name for Horsetail is Scouring Rush, because they're good for scrubbing and polishing things. I have used it for cleaning dishes when camping, as a toothbrush if I forget one and to polish wood after carving. Horsetails contain a mineral called silica, which is what makes them scrubby and is also what makes up a lot of our hair, teeth and nails. Some people drink tea made from Horsetail to strengthen their hair and fingernails.

> Kids call Horsetail "Lego plant," because you can pull apart the stem and then stick it back together.

> The Latin name for Horsetail, *Equisetum*, comes from the Latin name for "horse," which is *equus*.

Try This!

USE YOUR MEMORY

One person collects some things from nature—the top of a Horsetail plant, a pinecone, three different leaves, a cool stone or whatever else catches your eye. Anywhere between five and ten pieces works depending on the age of the players. The collector then arranges these items on a bandana and covers them with a second bandana. The players gather around the bandana, and the collector tells them how long they have to look at the items arranged beneath. Ten to thirty seconds usually works. Once their time is up, they have to go out and find all the items and arrange them in the same order on their own bandanas. The collector can be generous and give the players another peek. When all players have had a chance to get their arrangements as close as possible to the collector's, lift up the bandanas so the players can see what they got right and what they missed.

Variations: Once the players have their items arranged, give each one a turn to talk about one of their items. Or keep challenging the players' memories by rearranging the items while they close their eyes, and then the players try to spot what has been moved. You can play with themes like leaves, flowers or cones too.

Supplies needed:
- nature objects
- two bandanas or other pieces of cloth for each player

The memory game.

Horsetail **65**

Red Osier Dogwood

Cornus sericea

The white to pale-blue berries of Red Osier Dogwood are not good for us to eat, but they are great winter food for birds.

Description

This beautiful little shrub is common in the Northeast, growing wherever water is nearby. Red Osier Dogwood's deep-red bark and clusters of creamy white flowers make it easy to identify along riverbanks and in wetlands. Deer like to nibble the buds in spring, and creatures like chipmunks feast on the seeds contained in their bright white berries in the late summer and fall.

Cool Facts about Red Osier Dogwood

The long, smooth, red twigs of Dogwood are a favourite of basket weavers. If you're harvesting this plant for crafts like weaving, collect it in early spring before the leaf buds open. As the weather warms, the plant will put energy into growing strong leaves for photosynthesis. Snipping the twigs interrupts the Dogwood's life cycle. It's gentler on the plant to harvest just before it wakes up from winter.

Try This!

MAGIC WANDS

Supplies needed:
- a small stick
- small saw or hand pruners for cutting wands
- string or ribbons
- scissors

Making magic wands is fun for all ages. Take some time to wander and find just the right stick: a red twig of Osier Dogwood, a straight shoot of a Wild Rose, a patterned old beaver chew or a smooth, polished piece of driftwood. Keep your eyes open for feathers, leaves or other special things to tie on to your wand with the string or ribbon you brought along. When wands are finished, look at the magic word activity under Sundew (page 125) and cast some spells!

Making magic with our newly carved magic wands.

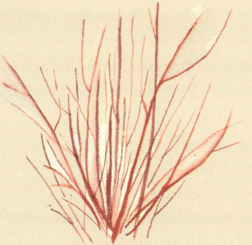

Red Osier Dogwood   **67**

Rose

Swamp Rose
Rosa palustris

Prickly Wild Rose
Rosa acicularis

Prairie Rose
Rosa setigera

Description

There are three main types of Wild Roses in this region: Swamp Rose, Prickly Wild Rose and Prairie Rose, which is considered at-risk. Of the one hundred or so Prairie Rose plant sites recorded, there are thought to be only sixty-eight left. They're the only native climbing rose in Canada and grow in the Carolinian zone, which is a rare habitat in southern Ontario that is home to over 500 sensitive species. This is also the only Rose that is **dioecious**, meaning one plant has female reproductive parts and another has male reproductive parts. Keep your eye out for the deep-pink flowers that come out in late May or early June. The Swamp Rose grows, like its name suggests, in swampy places. And the Prickly Wild Rose is the most common and easy to identify by the many small prickles that grow along its stems. The leaves of all these Roses are oval, sharply **serrated**, **alternate** and **deciduous**. In the winter, all three of these Roses

Rose hips.

68 Spring

have striking red stems. Roses like to grow in ditches, moist places where they can get some sun, at forest edges and in clearings.

"Wild Roses are beautiful and you can eat them!
— Beckett, age 11

All Rose family plants are edible.

Cool Facts about Wild Roses

Many of the fruits we eat are from the Rose family. This includes strawberries, apples, pears, plums, peaches, blackberries and raspberries. The hips of Wild Roses can be eaten or made into tea. One way to tell garden Roses from Wild Roses is to look at their thorns. Thorns of garden Roses are usually bigger and hooked.

Rose

Try This!

MAKE YOUR OWN ROSE-PETAL HONEY

Supplies needed:
- rose petals
- glass jar
- honey
- small pot
- strainer

In May, the air around roadside ditches, where thickets of Roses grow, smells sweet with the fragrance of both the flowers and the leaves. Making Rose-petal honey is a way to capture the scent and taste of late spring to enjoy in the middle of winter. All you need to do is go out and harvest Rose petals. Gently tug them from the flower, being on the lookout for bees at work pollinating. Make sure you leave enough flowers for the bees to enjoy. When you have collected a few big handfuls of petals, bring them home and lay them out in a basket or on a clean cloth for a day so that they can wilt. This releases the water in them so that when you add the honey, it won't ferment or go bad.

Put the Rose petals in a jar and cover them with honey. You will need to stir the petals around in the jar to make sure the honey is mixed in. Now let this jar sit on the windowsill for at least a month. Or you can leave it all the way until November, so when you open it, the scent of spring fills your winter day.

To separate the petals from the honey, place the jar with its lid on in a pot of water on the stove. Turn the heat to medium. When the

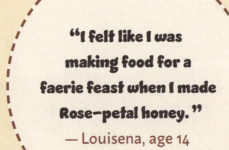

"I felt like I was making food for a faerie feast when I made Rose-petal honey."
— Louisena, age 14

70 Rose

water heats up, turn the stove down to low until the honey has liquified and can be strained off the Rose petals into a clean new jar. The leftover petals are delicious in desserts, on top of ice cream or stirred into tea. Yum!

Above left: Louisena makes Rose-petal honey.

Above right: A jar of Rose-petal honey.

Rose 71

Harvesting Tip

The hips of the Rose, which are the fruits, are best harvested after the first frost. The cold makes the vitamin C in the Rose hips more available. Dry the hips in a basket and add them to winter teas.

Note: The hairs that surround the seeds inside the hips of the Prickly Rose can cause an itchy bum on their way out. In some Indigenous languages, this plant is called Itchy Bum! It's great to nibble the fruit, but don't eat the whole hip. They will be fine whole in tea.

Astrid and Louisena collect Rose petals for Rose-petal honey.

72   Rose

Skunk Cabbage

Symplocarpus foetidus

Description

You might smell Skunk Cabbage before you see it. In the spring, when it sends up its weird red flowers, it also sends out its smell. I love the smell of a marsh full of Skunk Cabbage, but not everyone does. Perhaps I like it because it signals spring; Skunk Cabbage is one of the first flowers to come out in spring, even before its leaves do. The flowers look like large, mottled red-and-green candle flames, but technically, those are the **spathes** of the flower, and the actual flowers are arranged along the **spadix** inside. The shiny, waxy leaves will be small in the spring, growing larger until summertime, when some of these leaves get so long they're the size of a small child! Skunk Cabbage likes to grow in marshes, ditches, muddy stream beds and **bogs**.

Cool Facts about Skunk Cabbage

Did you know that Skunk Cabbage can melt snow?! The plant is able to create its own heat, maintaining a temperature of 21°C (or 70°F) all around it to melt ice or snow and allowing it to bloom in cold weather as early as March some years. The flowers and leaf buds are actually formed

Spring 73

Skunk Cabbage roots look like aliens from outer space!

The flowers of Eastern Skunk Cabbage coming out before the leaves.

underground in the autumn before they come out, and like bears, they hibernate underground waiting for spring before they emerge.

Even though Skunk Cabbage can be eaten, and has been eaten in the past when there was nothing else to eat, it's better not to because it contains little crystals, almost like fibreglass, that can be hard on your stomach. I do use the roots of Skunk Cabbage in cough medicine. The large, smooth waxy leaves were helpful in the days before stores. They can be used as plates, food wrap, trays for drying berries, racks for layering food in pit cooks, basket liners and cup holders. Deer love to eat Skunk Cabbage root tops, and if you walk through a marsh or muddy stream bed in the fall, you will see curious holes where the deer have dug for the roots.

Going on a Bear Hunt

On an autumn day, my friend Brad was wandering along the edge of a marsh, enjoying the wonderful smell of the Skunk Cabbage. He climbed up onto a fallen tree and saw such a big pile of **scat** that he thought it could only be bear poop! Bears are very rare in this area, so Brad was excited. When he told me, I was excited too!

The next day, we headed back to the marsh to have a look. As we squelched through the mud we talked all about where the bear could have come from and how it would have needed to cross highways to get here. I mentioned how some old timers had told me that they remember seeing bears come through this area in the fall, headed for the apple orchards nearby.

We wove through the thick Willow and stepped around the Horsetail and soon we were at the log. I climbed up and, sure enough, there was a huge pile of scat! It was full of grape skins, and as we looked closer, we saw there were also little bits of shells. Hmmm, do bears eat snails? And as we looked closer again, I thought, "That sure is a lot of poop, but is it really big enough to be bear poop?" And as we looked, asked questions and talked about it, our excitement started to fade.

Brad said solemnly, "Maybe this isn't bear poop." I nodded sadly. "Maybe I just wanted this to be bear poop," he said. I nodded. "Maybe I was so excited, I forgot to slow down and ask all the questions until I figured out what it really was." I nodded, then said "But maybe, just maybe, you found the biggest raccoon poop ever!"

Skunk Cabbage

Try This!

MARSH WANDER

People often stay out of marshes. They're wet, mucky, squishy and muddy. But what could be better?! Take off your shoes and socks, leave them at the edge and come explore. Step carefully between the giant Skunk Cabbage leaves and move silently through the tall grasses. You might see the smoothed-down grasses from a deer's bed. Enjoy the coolness of the mud on your feet and the melodic song of a Marsh Wren.

Enjoying the Cattails on our marsh wander.

Description

These tall **evergreen** trees with sturdy, downward-sloping branches are easy to find in parks and forests. Like all members of the Pine family, Spruce trees make two types of cones: one that bears pollen, and one that catches pollen. The seeds that grow in Spruce cones are a favorite food of Eastern Grey Squirrels. Look under a Spruce tree and you are likely to find piles of munched Spruce cones these rodents have left behind.

Spruce

Picea spp.

Look how big these Spruce cones are!

Spruce-tip jelly—yum!

Cool Facts about Spruce

The new bundles of soft, bright needles that emerge at the ends of the branches in spring are called Spruce tips. They're beloved by spring foragers for their flavour and medicine. They're aromatic and taste fresh and a little bit sour, like a Pine tree mixed with a citrus fruit. They're also high in vitamin C.

The sticky, fragrant sap inside Spruce trees is used as medicine to seal cuts and keep dirt from getting inside them. Hardened sap is called resin, and it's useful in tinder bundles for starting fires.

Harvesting Tip

All members of the *Picea* genus are edible. Find a place where you can taste different species. Which one do you like best? Remember that Spruce tips are the youngest part of the tree and will grow into new branches. Pick just one or two tips from each branch.

Try This!

MAKE YOUR OWN SPRUCE-TIP SYRUP

Supplies needed:
- Spruce tips
- jar
- brown sugar

Gather enough Spruce tips to fill your jar about ¾ full. Add a handful of Spruce tips to the jar, followed by a few spoonfuls of sugar. Repeat until the jar is full and give it a good shake to ensure that all of the Spruce tips are loosely covered in sugar. Let this mixture stand for a few days up to a week. Like magic, the sugar pulls the moisture out of the Spruce tips. The resulting deep-brown syrup is delicious and can be used wherever you would use Maple syrup. This syrup lasts a long time! Strain then store it in a jar with a tight-fitting lid in the fridge for up to four months.

A bucket full of Spruce tips.

Packing the Spruce tips and sugar into the jar to make syrup.

Spruce-tip syrup in the making.

Straining the Spruce tips.

Spruce

Stinging Nettle

Urtica dioica

Description

When Nettles come up in early spring, they're fuzzy, and sometimes almost purple. As they grow, their opposite, lance- to heart-shaped leaves get less fuzzy but are still sharply toothed and covered with fine hairs. They go to flower in May, making strange little clusters of greenish-brown balls that don't really look like flowers. These turn into light-brown droops of seed clusters in the summer. Eventually, the Nettles grow so tall, up to 3 metres (9 feet), that they droop over in graceful arches, with just a few leaves and seeds clinging to the stem. The stem of Nettle is square, but don't let this confuse you: it isn't in the Mint family. Nettle likes to grow in big patches in moist fields and clearings, under the dappled light of Aspens and Maples.

> "If you harvest Nettles without paying attention, they will get mad at you and sting you. But if you are careful, you can harvest a lot and you won't fall in."
> — Rueben, age 8

> What is cute, fuzzy and green when it's young, stings like a hundred red ants when it's middle-aged and curves gracefully like a dancer when it's old? Stinging Nettle, of course!

Cool Facts about Stinging Nettle

Even though Nettles sting, they're a superfood! They're packed with protein, calcium, magnesium, vitamin C and loads of other good things. The fibre from the stalks of Nettle is very strong and has been used by Indigenous people for making rope and twine. Huge nets would be made from the Nettle fibre for fishing and catching ducks.

> The sting from Nettles is made up of formic acid, the same thing that ants have in their sting!

Sophia harvests Stinging Nettle.

Stinging Nettle

Supplies needed:
- scissors
- basket or bag
- gloves

Harvesting Tip

Are you brave enough to eat Stinging Nettles? Well, here's a secret. They're delicious. And when the Nettles are cooked, blended or crushed, the stingers stop stinging. Harvest Nettle tops between late March and late May. Wear gloves if you must, but if you move slowly and carefully, you really don't need them. The stinging hairs are mostly on the underside of the leaves. With a pair of scissors or your knife, cut the Nettles' three-leaf nodes down, so that you are just taking the top three sets of leaves. Once you have a full bag, you can cut them up (now it's nice to wear gloves or oven mitts) and use them like spinach—but better. I like to make Nettle spanakopita, add them to omelettes or quiche, put them in smoothies, blend them into soups, and even add them to muffins. I also lay fresh Nettles out to dry in baskets or dry them in a food dehydrator and keep them to make a rich and nutritious tea all year. The seeds, when they're green and ripe, are a yummy, nutty-tasting snack, though sometimes they sting just a little.

> "Nettle makes good soup, and I love eating them."
> — Skye, age 11

> "We even put Nettles in pancakes, and they're sooo good."
> — Armas, age 9

82   Stinging Nettle

Try This!

NETTLE-SPANAKOPITA GRILLED CHEESE SANDWICHES

Directions:

1. Either plug in a panini press or heat a skillet over medium heat. Spread butter thinly on one side of each slice of bread.
2. In a medium skillet, heat olive oil over medium-high heat, add the garlic, and cook for four minutes, or until the garlic is golden-brown. Add Nettles and salt and pepper, and cook for a few minutes, until the Nettles are wilted and most of the moisture is cooked out. Add dill and feta, turn off heat and mix.
3. Assemble the sandwiches by placing two slices of bread butter side down on your press or pan, add one slice of cheese to each, then divide the Nettle mixture in half and place half on each slice. Top with the remaining two slices of cheese and slices of bread, butter side up.
4. If using a panini press, put the lid down and cook for about five minutes, or until golden and bubbly. If using a pan, flip after about five minutes, then cook on the other side for three minutes. Goes well with a mug of Dandelion coffee (page 54).

Ingredients:
- 1 Tbsp softened butter
- 4 slices good-quality whole grain bread
- 1 clove garlic, sliced thin
- 2 Tbsp olive oil
- 2 big handfuls of chopped Nettle leaves
- pinch each of salt and freshly cracked pepper
- 1 tsp chopped dill
- 2 ounces feta, crumbled
- 4 thin slices cheese, such as cheddar or Havarti

Makes two sandwiches

Adobe Stock, Walid

Stinging Nettle

Trillium

Trillium erectum

Trilliums come in shades from white, to pink, to scarlet.

> There are almost ten species of Trillium native to this region!

Description
Trillium gets its name from "tri," which means three. With their large, almost heart-shaped leaves, Trilliums are hard to miss among the other spring wildflowers. The flowers, which can range from white to pink to dark-red, also come in threes, and when the petals drop, there are three seed capsules left behind.

Cool Facts about Trillium
Trilliums are **myrmecochorous**, which is just a really big word that means "ants spread their seeds around!" Ants and Yellow Jackets are attracted to a part of the ripe seeds called the **elaiosome**, which is a fleshy white bit full of oils and

Try This!

LOOK AND ASK

This is a great game for practicing the art of questioning and a wonderful way to observe sensitive plant species. Have the group gather around a Trillium or any other plant you want to learn about. Go around the circle and have each person ask one question about the plant or make one observation. For example: "I see that there are subtle lines running along each petal" or "I wonder what type of root this plant has?" Take the time to look up the questions in your field guides at the end of the game.

Did you know that in the state of New York it's illegal to pick a Trillium? Trilliums are very fragile plants, and even wrecking one leaf can kill the entire plant. Because there aren't enough predators to eat deer these days, there are so many deer in some places that they're over-grazing on Trilliums and endangering them. They're also threatened by deforestation and disturbance from humans, so when you meet Trilliums, treat them with careful respect.

proteins. These insects like the elaiosome so much that they burrow into the fruit to take the seeds out and bring them home. This way, the seeds of Trilliums are spread throughout the forest. If you look within 2 metres (6 feet) of a Trillium patch, you are sure to find an ants' nest.

Trillium **85**

Trout Lily

Erythronium americanum

Trout Lily.

Description

Trout Lily is one of the first signs of spring in the **hardwood forests** of the Northeast. Its mottled brown-green leaves and bright yellow flowers can also be spotted emerging along moist paths and roadsides and in ditches. Trout Lily flowers droop down towards the ground to protect pollen from being washed away in the spring rains. Peek underneath and check out their deep-red stamens loaded with pollen.

Cool Facts about Trout Lily

Some people say Trout Lily got its name from the resemblance of its leaves to the speckled scales of Brook Trout. The Trout Lily also blooms at the same time that Trout fishing season opens in spring.

Try This!

TRANSFORMER PLANTS

Have you ever seen a Lily that can swim? What about a Cabbage that sprays you with stinky smells? Grab your sketchbook and coloured pencils and get creative. Draw some hybrid animal-plants and see what kind of crazy combos you can come up with. Next, look up a picture of your local species of Trout, and your local Lily species. Do you think these two species resemble each other? Draw these and compare them to the wild creatures your imagination created.

Harvesting Tip

Trout Lilies reproduce via underground structures called **corms** and form large groups called colonies. While all parts are edible, the most sustainable way to taste these plants is to pick a couple of leaves from each colony, leaving the corms to multiply. But be careful: Trout Lily can make some folks feel sick if they eat too many. With the help of an adult, harvest a couple leaves to taste and pay attention to how they feel in your belly.

Trout Lily

Spring Ephemeral Flowers

Like their neighbours Trillium, Bloodroot, Blue Cohosh and Hepatica, Trout Lilies are a special kind of native wildflower referred to as **spring ephemerals**. These wildflowers have adapted to their homes in the deciduous forests of the Northeast. When the snow melts, and the soil begins to warm, spring ephemerals emerge from under the leaf litter. They bloom for a short time compared to most flowers, allowing them to take advantage of the brief period of spring sunlight before the leaves of their neighbours, Maple and Beech, shade the forest floor once more. The leaves and flowers of spring ephemerals disappear by late spring, and the plants store their energy in their underground roots, bulbs and corms for the majority of the year. Spring ephemeral wildflowers reproduce slowly and many may only grow in Maple-Beech forests. Treat these delicate but powerful plants with respect and care.

Trout Lilies and Wild Leeks in a spring ephemeral wood.

Wild Ginger

Asarum canadense

Description

Wild Ginger grows close to the ground with many stems forming large mats of slightly fuzzy, heart-shaped leaves. The flowers come out in mid-spring and are a red-brown colour. They're often tucked in behind the leaves but are worth looking for because they're quite unusual, with three long squiggly petals. Wild Ginger likes to grow in moist, rich soil, often in the fallen leaves of deciduous trees, like Aspen or Beech.

Cool Facts about Wild Ginger

Aside from looking like they're from outer space, the flowers are also interesting because they're pollinated by flies and ants, rather than by bees! The flowers smell and look like rotten meat so that flies are attracted to them. But don't worry, the roots don't taste like rotten meat! As its name suggests, Wild Ginger roots taste kind of like the ginger you can buy at the grocery store. In the fall or spring, you can carefully dig up a root and use it to make yummy tea that is good for stomach aches or colds. It isn't quite as spicy as regular ginger, but it can still be used in its place in cooking.

> Ants carry the tiny black seeds of Wild Ginger around, accidentally planting them as they go. I often find large patches of Wild Ginger around ant hills.

Spring

Harvesting Tip

Only harvest Wild Ginger from a large, healthy patch. Take no more than one root per twenty plants. Gently pull aside the top layer of soil to expose the roots and then cut three inches of root between two nodes, so that the part left behind will continue to grow. Be sure to cover the roots back up with the soil you moved.

Too Much Ginger!

Many years ago, I was camping in the mountains with a bunch of friends. Somehow, we hadn't packed enough food for our week out in the woods. By the last three days, we were down to brown rice and oats. We thought we would spice up our plain food by adding some Wild Ginger to the rice while it cooked. This turned out pretty well, so the next morning, we also added Wild Ginger to our oatmeal. And then again to our rice for lunch. Well, after three days of eating Wild Ginger–flavoured every-thing, I couldn't wait to eat a hamburger. Nor could I bear to even think about Wild Ginger, let alone eat it again, for a long, long time!

Try This!

NATURAL VALENTINE'S DAY CARD

For a natural twist on Valentine's Day cards, pick one leaf from a healthy patch and take it home. You can trace its outline for a nice heart to make Wild Ginger valentines.

Making a Wild Ginger valentine.

Plant Tag

This is a fun way to learn the names of plants. This game can be played almost anywhere outside, from a school field to a thick forest. The person who is "it" stands in the middle of a specific area and calls out the name of a plant, shrub or tree growing nearby. Everyone else stands at the edge of the given area and has to run to the plant that is called without being tagged by the person who is "it." The runners are safe once they're (gently) touching the plant. If a runner is tagged, they join the "it" person in the middle. The game is over when everyone is caught.

Plant tag is great for all levels of learners, with the obvious plants, like trees, being easy to identify, and smaller green or dried-up plants, like St. John's Wort in the winter, being harder. People will follow the person who knows the plant being called, thereby teaching each other. This game can be played using Latin names or by describing the plant.

Playing plant tag.

Allium tricoccum

Description

It's a welcome sight for our winter-weary eyes: Wild Leeks unfurling their leaves in hardwood forests in the early spring, bringing the dull, brown forest floor to life in carpets of green. This small plant is composed of two or three smooth, broad leaves with narrow reddish-purple stems. Under the soil, white bulbs that look like little onions are protected by a papery, purple sheath. Just as their leaves begin to die back, the plant sends up a single stalk bearing small white flowers. In the fall, all that remains visible of these plants is their thin brown stem bearing a ring of lovely seeds that resemble tiny black pearls.

A field of Wild Leeks in flower.

Spring

Cool Facts about Wild Leeks

A happy, healthy patch of Wild Leeks.

The fresh, spicy flavour of Wild Leeks is a beloved harbinger of spring for many plant lovers. This potent native plant is a cousin of the onions and garlic in your cupboard (also members of the *Allium* genus) and shares their pungent, aromatic flavour. Wild Leeks are used in cooking much the same way you would use a green onion or shallot.

Like many ephemerals that grow in hardwood forests in early spring, Wild Leeks reproduce slowly. Really, really slowly! A Wild Leek plant can take up to seven years to create seeds, and seeds can take several years to germinate.

Harvesting Tip

Freshly harvested Wild Leek.

Unfortunately, the popularity of Wild Leeks as an ingredient has led to over-harvesting, causing them to be endangered in parts of the Northeast. In some places, it's even illegal to pick them. Check with knowledgeable adults in your region to find out if you can responsibly harvest this plant. If so, be sure to take only one leaf per plant and only a small amount of leaves from each patch you find. Never harvest the bulbs or the plant won't grow back next spring.

Wild Leek

Try This!

WILD LEEK PESTO

You can make this spicy pesto each spring to savour on pasta, toast or eggs. Instead of using a recipe, let your taste buds be your guide. Wash a couple of handfuls of Wild Leek leaves (not bulbs) and combine them in a food processor with olive oil and salt to taste. I also like to add Romano cheese (or any hard cheese), walnuts or pumpkin seeds and a dash of lemon juice if I have them on hand. Pulse until the mixture forms a paste, taste and add ingredients to adjust the flavour as you like. A little goes a long way!

Supplies needed:
- Wild Leek leaves
- food processor
- olive oil
- salt
- Romano cheese
- walnuts or pumpkin seeds
- lemon

Make your own Wild Leek pesto!

Wild Leek

Spring Scavenger Hunt

1. Find the sign of one creature who lives where you are.
2. Collect four plants that are edible and show them to a knowledgeable adult before you eat them.
3. Find a yellow flower, a white flower and a purple or pink flower.
4. Listen to a bird call, then imitate it for your adult or friend.
5. Collect five different leaves that have just started growing.
6. With your finger, dig a little hole in the ground. Can you see any bugs?
7. Can you find a Fern uncurling? What kind is it?
8. What insects can you see or hear? Are they collecting pollen or nectar from a nearby flower?
9. Smell three flowers. Which one smells the sweetest?

Spring on the riverbank.

Wild Leek

Summer

Summer is a time of long days and heat, which brings more flowers and ripens fruit and seeds. It's a season of yummy berries to eat and long days to play outside.

Hunting for Milkweed in tall grasses.

Bee Balm

Monarda fistulosa

Description

When Bee Balm is flowering, it lets itself be known by bright-red to dark-pink flowers that look like a cool hairdo atop a normal Mint plant. Bee Balm is in the Mint family, and like all Mint plants, it has a square stem, lance-shaped opposite leaves and is very fragrant.

Cool Facts about Bee Balm

With purple, scarlet and fuschia blooms, Bee Balm, as its name suggests, attracts bees as well as butterflies. It is wonderful and easy to grow in gardens and makes a great companion for Milkweed, which feeds and hosts Monarch butterflies. Because Bee Balm keeps its flowers late into the summer, it offers pollinators much needed late-summer food. Bee Balm has been used as tea by Indigenous People of this region for thousands of years for coughs, colds, flus, upset tummies and as a wash to help heal infections.

Summer

Try This!

PICK YOUR OWN BEE BALM TEA

You can make a yummy and healing tea with this plant! Anytime between late June and early September, find a patch of Bee Balm growing in a clean area. It grows in moist fields and creeksides. Use a pair of scissors to snip off the plant just above the bottom leaves. Many Mints will regrow from the node below the cut. When you get home, bunch the plants together and tie them with string or rubber band and hang the bundle to dry. You can also take the leaves and flowers off the stem and lay them in a basket or dehydrator until they're dry. Do the "snap crunch" test to make sure they're completely dry before storing them in an airtight jar or Ziploc bag. (There is nothing sadder than finding mouldy leaves when you want tea!)

To make the tea, place 1 tablespoon of dried leaves in a teapot or mug and top with boiling water. Steep with a lid on for ten minutes. If you don't cover your tea while it's steeping, all the good oils and the flavour will evaporate! Add a little honey if you like.

Supplies needed:
- Bee Balm
- scissors
- string or rubber band
- jar or Ziploc bag
- kettle
- teapot or mug

A rusty-patched Bumble Bee collects pollen from a Bee Balm blossom.

The first time I met Bee Balm in the wild, there was magic in the air. I was setting up my tent just as the sun was going down on an early August day next to the Grand River. I had come to a little town in the area to see where my great-great grandmother had lived. When I finished laying out my sleeping bag, I opened the zipper of my tent to crawl out again, and there was the most magical view I had ever seen. Pink, peach and purple light from the sunset was reflected in the slow-moving river, and this same light hovered over a vast field of Bee Balm, making the soft mauve of the flowers splendid in the evening light. There had been thunder and lightning that afternoon, and now with the rain evaporating in the hot evening, the air was misty and filled with the fragrance of the Bee Balm. I soaked up the colours and sweet smells. And then! Oh delight! Out came the fireflies, like twinkling insect stars floating and winking among the Bee Balm! I sat there in pure wonder listening to the shush of the river and then the distant sound of coyotes yipping in the night. They too were out enjoying the beauty of the place my great-great grandmother once knew.

Common Milkweed

Asclepias syriaca

Description
There are many species of Milkweed that grow in the Great Lakes region. The small five-petalled flowers grow in clusters, creating sweet-smelling balls. The plump seed pods form unusual shapes that ripen and burst open with the white fluff of their seeds. Milkweed is named after the white, latex liquid that can be found in the stems.

Cool Facts about Milkweed
Milkweed is an important plant for pollinators, from bees and wasps to butterflies. In fact, they're the main food source for Monarch caterpillars. These caterpillars have evolved alongside Milkweed so that they can ingest the toxins in the plant without being harmed. The toxins then make the caterpillars poisonous to birds and other predators, who won't dare eat the caterpillars. Smart, hey? The problem is that when you only have one thing to eat, that thing better be available, otherwise you will starve. That is why it's important to grow Milkweed!

Summer   101

The downy soft fluff of Milkweed seeds waiting to blow away on the wind.

Did you know that Milkweed fluff can be used to make stuffing for pillows and winter coats?

Harvesting Tip

If you want to try eating Milkweed pods, it's best to collect them when they're young and green. When they're any bigger than an inch long or have started to split, they will be no good. When you open the pod up, the newly forming seeds inside should be totally white. If they have started to turn brown at all, they will be unpleasant to eat. Cut the pods into pieces about 3 centimetres (1 inch) long and cook them as you might cook Green Beans or Okra.

Common Milkweed

Try This!

GROW A BUTTERFLY GARDEN

Monarch butterflies are beautiful to see as they arrive by the thousands in the early summer. They travel over 5,000 miles, all the way from Mexico, and are the only insect to migrate like birds do! In the old days, it was said that the sky would be so full of butterflies that they would block out the sun. These days, there are fewer and fewer butterflies because their habitats are being destroyed by city sprawl and pesticides. You can help the butterflies by planting more food for them. Here is how.

In the fall, when the Milkweed pods have turned brown, head out with a paper bag to harvest the seed pods that have not yet split open. Leave the ones with the white fluff sticking out for the wind to plant. Choose pods that are dry and brown but unopened. When you get home, open the pods over a big bowl. You will find little brown seeds on the inside that can be separated from the white floss. Discard the floss and save the seeds.

These seeds can be planted out in the fall by spreading them on freshly raked earth in a sunny place. Lightly cover the seeds with soil and water them. Be sure to make a little sign so you remember what you planted there (spring is still a long way off). If you prefer to plant them in the spring, store the seeds in a well-labeled envelope in the fridge. This is like a pretend winter for seeds, which need a cold period or **stratification** before they will grow in the spring.

Supplies needed:
- Milkweed seed pods
- paper bag
- large bowl

Monarch butterlies are dependant on Milkweed flowers as a food for their caterpillars.

Common Milkweed   103

Ghost Pipe

Monotropa unifloria

Description

You may come upon a cluster of Ghost Pipe in some old forest one day and say "What the heck is this?!" This small white fleshy plant belongs to the Wintergreen **clan** in the Heath family. When it first pushes up through the rich soil where it likes to grow, it looks almost like some curled-up creature. Then it unfurls and shows its white-and-black-edged flowers that droop over like bells. When Ghost Pipe goes to seed, the flowers turn up to become seed capsules, and the whole plant becomes brown and dried out.

Cool Facts about Ghost Pipe

This is a weird plant. It almost doesn't quite look like a plant because it's not green. What is it? Ghost Pipe is actually a **parasite** plant, meaning it feeds off another living plant instead of making its own food, like most plants do through photosynthesis. In the case of Ghost Pipe, this is done by connecting its small roots to **mycelium** (the underground network of fungi roots in the ground), which is then connected to the roots of **coniferous** trees. This may seem like a roundabout way for this little plant to feed itself, and indeed, it needs a healthy old forest with lots of decaying matter and mycelium to do this. Because of this, you will only find it in mature woods.

Summer

Gather 'Round the Ghost Pipe

I find this plant so interesting to look at. Out walking with a friend one day, I spotted a large patch of Ghost Pipe growing beside the trail in a popular park. "Come check this out," I said to my friend. There we were, lying on our bellies looking at the Ghost Pipe, when my daughter's piano teacher happened to walk by with her whole family. "What are you looking at?" they asked. And so I explained all about this strange white plant. Soon enough, they were down on their bellies looking at the Ghost Pipe too. Even the grandpa! A few minutes later, the local doctor, who likes to walk his fluffy dog through the park, came along. "What are you looking at?" he asked. Soon he was down on his knees looking at the Ghost Pipe too. There we were—a paramedic, a teacher, a piano teacher and her whole family and a doctor—all gathered 'round this strange little plant. We never did see any ghosts, but I bet the Ghost Pipe felt pretty special!

"That's weird! Is it even a plant?!"
— Timon, age 8

Harvesting Tip

DON'T. This plant is rare and sensitive and should only be looked at and not picked.

Blue dog found this Ghost Pipe.

Ghost Pipe

Try This!

UP CLOSE AND PERSONAL

Astrud looks at the world up close.

Supplies needed:
- notepad
- pencil
- magnifying glass (if you have one)

There is so much to see right in front of us that we often miss things as we walk around. Even from five feet up I miss a lot. Get right down on your belly to see the world of the small. Choose a spot of your liking; it can be in a meadow, a lawn, a thick forest, the lakeside or even a crack in the pavement. With sticks or string, square off a space about 30 centimetres by 30 centimetres (1 foot by 1 foot). This is now your universe. Begin your exploration on the surface. Notice how many plants grow there. Can you see any bugs or insects? Are there any signs of mammal life? Make notes in your book. Sketch what you see. Now look closer. Dig down into the soil or sand, making a little opening so you can see the world that is usually hidden to us. What is the soil like? Is it sandy or clay-rich? Can you see any white mycelium threads? What tiny creatures live below the surface? Spend a good, quiet twenty minutes here in this little but vast universe. When you get up, the rest of the world will never look the same.

Ghost Pipe

Description

Burdock can grow as tall as me (1.5 metres, or 5 feet) when it's in seed. It has large, soft arrow- to lance-shaped leaves that grow close to the ground before sending up its stem in the spring. The flowers of Burdock almost look like Thistles; they're reddish-pink and covered with sharp spikes, lacking any obvious petals. Burdock was introduced from Europe where it has a long history of being used for medicine. It likes to grow in moist, rich soil in fields, next to gardens and on roadsides.

Common Burdock

Arctium minus

Cool Facts about Burdock

The flower and seed heads are very sticky and prickly. The plant uses this as a method to spread itself around. Walk through a patch of Burdock and you will get some seeds stuck to your pants. Dogs and sheep get the seeds tangled in their coats. So with our help, the plant can move around. The little hooks on the end of the "spikes" on the seeds inspired the invention of Velcro. In Japan, Burdock roots are eaten just like any other root vegetable.

Burdock is in the Aster family. Can you figure out why it's related to Dandelion?

Summer

Never stick Burdock burrs in someone's hair. They knot even more than chewing gum, and I have had to cut them out of many long, beautiful locks!

Try This!

STEALTH BURDOCK TAG

Collect some Burdock seeds. As the day goes along, the challenge is to stick a burr on your friend's or instructor's back without them noticing. Keep your owl eyes on—someone may try to stick one on you!

Sneaky Burdock burrs!

Breah and the Burdock burrs.

108   Common Burdock

Field Mint

Mentha arvensis

Description

Like all plants in the Mint family, Field Mint has a square stem. It likes to grow on stream banks among sedges and grasses with its roots sometimes right in the water. The minty-smelling lance-shaped leaves are opposite, soft and lightly toothed. In the summer, Field Mint has pale-pink flowers that grow like little clusters of trumpets from where the leaves come out of the stem.

Cool Facts About Field Mint

Mint contains a sweet, spicy compound called menthol that causes a cooling effect in your mouth and on skin, so when you consume it cold, as in iced tea, it makes you feel cool. But if you drink it in a hot tea, it can actually make you sweat, the same way spicy foods can.

> "Field Mint makes really yummy tea!"
> — Zaylia, age 7

Summer 109

Try This!

SUN TEA

Supplies needed:
- A few handfuls of Mint
- large jar
- water
- scissors or knife

A super-easy way to make tea in the summer is with the sun! All you need is a large glass jar, a sunny spot, clean water and Mint! Cut the plant at the base, then snip or rip the leaves up and put them in your jar. Put the lid on the jar and place it in a sunny spot for two to three hours. When you come back, strain out the leaves. Chill the tea in the fridge if you want iced tea—perfect on a hot day!

The Missing Mint Mystery

One day, the kids and I spent the morning gathering Mint and Raspberries to make a special tea. We decided that a sunny meadow in the park would be the best place to let it steep while we went off to explore the cool banks of a creek. When we came back, the jar was gone! We were so disappointed. "Perhaps a raccoon took it," one kid said. "Or a raven swooped down and flew away with it," said another. "I think a UFO came and beamed it up," someone else offered. We never did find our tea, in my favourite big Mason jar too, but we hope whoever found it enjoyed the delicious wild tea!

Gabby and Margret harvesting Field Mint. Field Mint is best picked just before it flowers in early summer.

110   Field Mint

Fireweed

Epilobium angustifolium

Description

Fireweed has alternate lance-shaped leaves all the way up the stem, ending in a spire of bright magenta flowers at the top. The flowers have four petals. When the petals fall off, Fireweed makes pods full of white fluffy seeds. When the pods burst open, this fluff will float over clear cuts, recently burned areas and clearings.

Cool Facts about Fireweed

Fireweed likes to grow where the environment has been **disturbed**. It's like nature's bandage, healing the land by using its roots to hold the soil in place when trees and other plants have been taken away. The sea of pink flowers brings beauty to places that otherwise look ravaged from clear cutting or burns. Fireweed is also edible; the young shoots can be eaten like asparagus. A flavourful tea rich in vitamin C can be made from the leaves. Fireweed flowers midsummer, and many beekeepers bring their bees to gather the nectar from these flowers, which makes much of the honey you buy from the store.

> I bet you have had Fireweed honey without even knowing it!

Summer 111

Left: A magnificent magenta bowl of Fireweed petals.

Right: Make Fireweed jelly by cooking the petals down and then following any jelly recipe.

"I like this tea. It is refreshing. I think it would make good iced tea on a hot day."
— Naomi, age 10

Harvesting Tip

To eat the shoots in spring, just cut the plant at its base, peel off the outer layer of skin and eat it raw or steam it like asparagus. To make tea, harvest the plant before it goes to flower or right at flowering time. Bunch the stems together, tie them and hang the bundle to dry. Once dry, you can pull off the leaves and flowers and keep these for tea.

Description

Oxeye Daisy, of the Aster family, looks like a daisy should, with white petals around a yellow centre. It's a tall daisy, up to your knees, with alternate lobed leaves about 3 centimetres (1 inch) long coming off the stem. One plant has many stems and flowers. Before the stalks grow, the plant is just a round cluster of leaves close to the ground. Oxeye Daisy thrives in fields, on roadsides and in open cleared areas.

Cool Facts about Oxeye Daisy

Oxeye Daisy is native to Europe, but now widely spread across North America. Birds like Finches like to eat the seeds in the late summer.

Nibble This!

The leaves of Oxeye Daisy are edible, and the young leaves are especially sweet, tasting a bit like vanilla. You can munch them as a snack or add them to a salad.

Oxeye Daisy

Leucanthemum vulgare

"Oxeye Daisies look like fried eggs on a stem."
— Breah, age 10

Summer

Try This!
....

THE LONGEST DAISY CHAIN EVER!

Oxeye Daisies make great daisy chains. Just use your fingernail or the tip of a sharp knife to make a slit two inches from the end of the stem, then slide in another daisy and make a slit in the end of that stem and so on. Work as a team to make the longest chain ever!

Rueben, Maya and Breah made a 25-foot-long daisy chain!

114   Oxeye Daisy

Plantain

(Ribwort)

English Plantain or Longleaf
Plantago lanceolata

Common or Oval Leaf Plantain
Plantago major

Description

There are two kinds of Plantain. English Plantain (*Plantago lanceolata*) has long lance-shaped leaves. Common Plantain (*Plantago major*) has round to oblong leaves. Both of these plants have deeply **parallel-veined** leaves, which give them their other name, Ribwort. They're low-growing plants. In the summer, they send up many stems with very un-flower-like flowers. These flowers form small green, then brown, heads on the stems, and then send out what looks like a little white halo around each flower head. Plantain likes to grow in moist rich soil, in gardens, meadows, cracks in the sidewalk and open clearings.

Common Plantain.

Summer 115

Breah harvests Plaintain leaf for making oil.

Plantain has been called "White Man's Footstep" because it was noticed that the plant grew wherever the first European settlers passed through.

Cool Facts about Plantain

Plantain is a gently soothing healing plant with **styptic** properties similar to Yarrow, which means it stops bleeding. The kids in my nature school know to look for Plantain right away if someone gets a Bee or Nettle sting. "Found some!" Zaylia calls as she comes running over with three leaves to give to Gabby for her sting.

Try This!
. . . .

MAKE YOUR OWN PLANTAIN SALVE

Supplies needed:
- Plantain leaves
- olive, avocado, apricot kernel or another kind of whole oil
- old newspaper
- some small jars
- beeswax
- small saucepan you don't mind getting oily
- kitchen scale
- measuring cup
- lavender essential oil (optional)

Measuring the Plantain oil for making salve.

Plantain   117

Naomi and Chantel pour Plantain salve.

Plantain salve is good to have on hand for those times when you can't go pick some. It's healing both to bug bites and Nettle stings, but also to dry and chapped skin, rashes, diaper rash, eczema and slow-healing cuts. Making the salve is a two-step process.

First, harvest some Plantain leaves when they're fresh. Then make an oil from them following the directions for Cottonwood bud oil (page 59). Alternatively, you can dry the leaves and make an oil in your blender by adding seven parts of oil to one part of dried Plantain leaves. Blend the leaves in the oil for about fifteen minutes. The blender will heat up the oil and extract the medicine from the Plantain.

Be careful: the blender might be hot. Strain the plant bits from the oil. Now you are ready to make the salve:

1. Lay down old newspaper on the counter to make cleaning up easy.
2. Have your small jars clean, dry and ready to use.
3. You can add a drop or two of Lavender essential oil into the bottom of each jar if you like. This is also good for burns, bites and wound-healing, plus it smells good and keeps the salve from spoiling.
4. Put your strained oil in a small pot on low heat on the stove. 125 millilitres (½ cup) of oil will make about 150 millilitres (5 ounces) of salve.
5. Cut your beeswax into small bits so it melts faster. You need 28 grams (1 ounce) of beeswax for every 250 millilitres (1 cup) of oil you use.

6. Let the wax dissolve into the oil on the stove, stirring once in a while and making sure it doesn't come to a boil.
7. When the wax is completely melted into the oil, you can carefully pour this into your jars. You can also pour it into a measuring cup with a spout to make pouring into your small jars easier.
8. Let the jars of salve cool where they are without moving them.
9. When they're completely cool, put their lids on and make some decorative labels, maybe with a drawing of the plants you used.
10. Your equipment will need to be washed with very hot water and lots of soap to get the oil and wax off!
11. Carry your Plantain salve in your hiking bag or first aid kit, use it at home or give it away for gifts.

Our finished Plantain salve!

Plantain

St. John's Wort

Hypericum perforatum

Description

This beautiful, bright and weedy plant is originally from Eurasia. The small yellow flowers bloom around the summer solstice and look like little golden suns, with the stamens shooting outward like rays of sunshine. When you hold the small oval leaves up to the light, you can see why the Latin name is *perforatum*, which means "perforated," because of the way the light shines through tiny holes in the leaves. This plant is a **perennial** that dies back in the winter.

Cool Facts about St. John's Wort

St. John's Wort is named so because it was traditionally gathered at the time of the mid-summer festival. When Christians took over the pagan holidays, they gave them new names and called the summer solstice the Feast of St. John. The flowers have a long history of being used for medicine, including as a treatment for mild depression, acting like little suns to lift the mood. In the old days, this plant was thought to ward

> "Wort" is an Old English word for a healing plant. Don't worry, this plant won't give you warts, and it may even take them away!

120   Summer

off evil, and it was hung above doorways and in animals' stalls. Plants used this way were called *fuga daemonum* in Latin, which means "demon-flight." The flowers of St. John's Wort, when pressed between your fingers, make a beautiful dark-red colour that will stain your skin. St. John's Wort is toxic to sheep and cows, causing them to get sick and sunburn more easily. Keep your eyes out when you harvest this plant; there are beautiful metallic beetles who live in the flowers and shimmer like tiny jewels.

Harvesting Tip

St. John's Wort grows on roadsides and in wastelands, so make sure you are harvesting from places that are free of pesticides and pollutants. Only harvest the tops of the plants and make sure you leave enough flowers for the insects.

St. John's Wort, which flowers around the summer solstice, looks like a thousand small suns.

Try This!

MAKE YOUR OWN HEALING OIL

Supplies needed:
- a handful of St. John's Wort flowers and buds
- a small jar
- olive oil
- strainer

Caution: Do not put on oil before going out into the sun. It can cause some people to be more sensitive to sunburn.

Carefully harvest just the flowers and buds of St. John's Wort from a healthy patch of plants until you have a handful. Place the flowers in a jar, cover with extra-virgin olive oil and put on the lid. Make sure the jar and the lid are totally dry, otherwise your oil will mould. Let this oil sit on your windowsill for two to six weeks. Over time, the oil magically turns from gold to deep-red. When you are ready, strain the flowers from the oil. The oil can be used on its own or turned into a salve following the Plantain Salve recipe (page 117). Use this oil on sprains, sore muscles, warts, shingles or areas that have suffered nerve damage.

Notice the beautiful deep red colour of this healing St. John's Wort oil.

122 St. John's Wort

Sundew

Drosera rotundifolia

Description

Sundew is an insect-eating plant that grows where it's wet, on lake and marsh edges and in Sphagnum Moss bogs. I often see it growing on trees that have fallen into lakes and become like little islands with plants growing from them. Sundew is a small plant, easy to overlook at first, just as tall as your longest finger. It grows in clusters on logs or moss. The leaves are on the ends of the stems and are flat and round with sticky tentacles covered in clear goo protruding from the leaves. This is where the flies get trapped and eaten. In the summer, Sundew makes little white flowers that only open in bright sun.

Cool Facts about Sundew

Sundew is related to the Venus Fly Trap (*Dionaea muscipula*), and what is cooler than a **carnivorous** insect-eating plant?! Sundews eat flies

> "If I could turn myself into any plant, I would be a Sundew and eat dragons! Or dragonflies at least."
> — Rueben, age 9

Summer 123

Although Sundew has no teeth, I have seen them eat dragonflies!

Harvesting Tip

Don't pick them. These plants are rare and grow in sensitive ecosystems.

One of the best ways to get up close to Sundew without disturbing their habitats is to canoe or swim to where they grow on logs fallen into a lake or marsh. You might catch them eating flies! I took this picture when I took off my shoes and socks and balanced on a fallen Cedar log.

I wouldn't want to be this damsel fly being devoured by the Sundew!

and other insects to add to their diet because they have a hard time photosynthesizing or making food from the sun. They do this by trapping insects in their sticky pads; a chemical in the goo causes the insect to break down and be absorbed by the plant. These tiny and uncommon plants have many uses: they can help remove warts, curdle milk or make cheese, and soothe coughs. Eating Sundew supposedly turns your pee a different colour.

124   Sundew

Try This!

MAGIC SPELLS

Have you ever said the Latin names of plants out loud? Doesn't "*Drosera rotundifolia!*" sound like a spell from *Harry Potter*? Especially with an exclamation mark at the end. Perhaps it turns you into a fly, or makes your enemy dissolve, or cures warts, or even makes someone fall in love with you. Can you think of any other magic spells using Latin names? What about "*Asarum canadense!*" (the Latin name for Wild Ginger)? Maybe this spell makes a person hot all over, turns your enemies into slugs or cures tummy aches. There are endless magic spells to be said aloud. They are best accompanied by a magic wand (see the Red Osier Dogwood activity on page 67). But be careful to follow the rule all magic makers have to follow: "do unto others as you would have done unto you," meaning don't do anything to anyone that you wouldn't want done to you!

Can you think of any magic spells?

Tansy

Tanacetum vulgare

The golden buttons of Tansy.

Description

Tansy, originally from Eurasia, is in the Aster family. It begins as a cluster of feathery, Fern-like leaves and grows tall, sturdy stalks in early summer. By July, round, flat flowers that look like bright yellow buttons sit atop the stalks. Tansy likes full sun and grows along stream banks and roadsides.

Cool Facts about Tansy

Sniff a bunch of Tansy fronds and you will be welcomed with a sweet, musky fragrance. This is because Tansy is very high in essential oils. These oils make Tansy good for medicine but only if used correctly—too much and they can be toxic. One of these essential oils is called Thujone, which is also found in Cedar trees. Thujone can be used as an insect repellent and turned into a tea that treats parasites, but if it's consumed in large amounts, it can hurt your liver. In the old days, people wore Tansy in their shoes, believing this would keep diseases like malaria away, and when someone died, they would be buried with Tansy to help keep insects away from the body. Today, Tansy makes a great companion plant in gardens because insects don't like it and will stay away from it. Plant it near potato or squash to ward off unwanted guests.

Try This!

LESS AND MORE

Some plants are funny because they can be both medicine and poison. We need to be careful how we use plants like Tansy. If you use too much, it can hurt you, but if you use just the right amount, it can be helpful. Make a list of other things like this. What can hurt you if you have too much? What can help if you have just a little? Try putting these things into categories of "Less" and "More:" water, ice cream, Tansy, YouTube, Dandelion. What else can you think of?

Harvesting Tip

Before you handle or touch Tansy, try rubbing a piece on a tiny patch of skin and wait a few minutes. Some people have an allergic reaction that causes a little rash. It's not serious, but it's best for these people not to handle it too much. Harvest Tansy when it's in full flower and hang it in the kitchen or pantry to keep flies away. You can also hang the full plant to dry and add it to campfires—the smoke can help keep mosquitoes away.

Tansy **127**

Wild Raspberry

Rubus idaeus

Description

Wild Raspberries look just like garden raspberry plants, with deeply veined leaves that are dusty silver on the undersides. They're called Caneberries (along with Blackberries and Boysenberries) because they grow along woody canes instead of on vines. The canes or stems of the bush are green to light-blue with small prickles. They flower (pale-green blossoms that are almost unnoticeable) and bear red berries in the early summer of their second year, then die off in fall, making way for new canes to emerge in spring.

Cool Facts about Wild Raspberry

Because Raspberries like to grow in sunny, clear areas like trail sides, they make an excellent snack while you are out hiking or biking. There are no poisonous berries that look like Wild Raspberry, so you can feel free to munch away with confidence as long as you leave some for the bears, coyotes and other humans.

> Did you know that a Raspberry is not just one berry but that each little bump is a berry on its own, each containing one seed?

Summer

Try This!

RASPBERRY SMOOTHIE

Ingredients:
- 1 cup fresh or frozen Raspberries
- 1 cup whole yogourt, milk or non-dairy milk of your choice
- 1 banana, sliced
- 1 tsp orange juice concentrate
- 1 cup water

Makes four smoothies to share with your friends.

Place all ingredients in a blender, blend until smooth and serve right away!

Yum!

> My dog loves to eat Raspberries off the bush. Does yours? It's so cute to see him nibble them daintily from the bush, but not so cute when he eats them all!

Wild Raspberry

Wild Strawberry

Fragaria virginiana

Woodland Strawberry

Fragaria vesca

Description

Wild Strawberries look much like their bigger garden-variety cousins. They have soft green leaves in sets of three, white flowers with yellow centres and, in early summer, small heart-shaped red fruits. Strawberries spread by sending out **runners**, long stems that creep across the ground finding new spots to grow. Like so many yummy fruits, Strawberries are in the Rose family.

Cool Facts about Wild Strawberries

Have you ever looked closely at a Strawberry? Unlike most fruits who hide their seeds inside the flesh of the fruit, Strawberries wear their seeds on the outside. One little Strawberry can have a thousand tiny seeds decorating its fruit. When animals eat the fruit, they poop out the seeds, thus possibly planting a new Strawberry patch somewhere else.

Strawberry Wolves

It was a windy day in Northern Ontario when I found the most amazing patch of Wild Strawberries ever. They were growing next to a little creek that seeped out from a thick Spruce forest. As I crawled around on my hands and knees, I was delighted every time I found a berry and popped it into my mouth. After hiking for days with only raisins for fruit, the fresh sweetness of the Strawberries was amazing.

I was so lost in hunting for berries, that I was surprised all of a sudden by the sound of footsteps. Not the sound of a human's heavy two-footed trudge. It was the sound of four light feet. I turned, and there was a wolf running right toward me! Surprised by the wolf's sudden appearance, I blurted out, "Hey, wolf! Stop!" And it did. As quickly as it had been running toward me, it turned right back around and went the way it had come.

The wolf was about as tall as my thigh and had scraggly light-grey-and-blond fur. My heart beat quickly, for although I knew wolves very rarely hurt humans, it was still startling to have a wild animal run right toward me. The wind had been blowing my scent away from it, and I had been crouched down, so the wolf had neither smelled nor seen me. As I looked around, wondering if it would come back, I noticed something I would have seen earlier had my attention not just been on the Strawberries. About 3 metres (15 feet) away from me, just down the bank, was the mostly eaten skeleton of an animal. Gosh! I was right in the wolf's kitchen. Feeling kind of bad about interrupting the wolf's dinnertime, I reluctantly headed up the creek to find a campsite.

I had only gone a few paces when I heard the sound of footsteps again on the bank. Sure enough, another wolf was heading full tilt straight at me! Startled, again I yelled out,

Nibble This!
. . . .

Although they're small, Wild Strawberries are packed with flavour! The best way to spot them is lying on your belly or crawling around on your hands and knees, so you can find the little red fruits hiding under their leaves. Some people like to eat them one at a time, and some people like to fill their palms and then pop the handful in their mouths for a big burst of yumminess!

Wild Strawberry   **131**

"Wild Strawberries are one of my favourite plants because they're juicy and sweet."
— Harriet, age 10

"Stop, wolf!" Equally surprised to see me, this wolf, who had black fur, also turned around and disappeared into the forest.

With a racing heart, I did my best to set up my camp for the night. Every time the river gurgled or the wind blew on my tent, I was sure it was another wolf running down the bank toward me. Even as I tried to sleep, one ear stayed open for the sound of an animal's approach. At some point in the night I must have drifted off to sleep, because just as the dawn chorus of birdsong started up, I was awoken by the sound of footsteps going past my tent. I lay still and quiet, hoping I wasn't in the way of the wolves. Were they going to gnaw on that skeleton?

When I finally crawled out of my tent after a rough sleep, I went to see if the wolves had moved the carcass. They hadn't, and there was no sign that the wolves had touched it in the night. So I went to find some Strawberries for breakfast and what did I see? There were wolf prints all around the Strawberry patch! So this is what they had wanted all along. The sweet goodness of ripe Wild Strawberries!

The delicate harvest of Wild Strawberries, just before the wolves came.

132   Wild Strawberry

Willow

Salix spp

Black Willow
Salix nigra

Sandbar Willow
Salix exigua

Shining Willow
Salix lucida

Description

There are over twenty types of Willows in the Great Lakes region! Learning to tell them apart takes a lifetime of getting to know Willows. Here are three common varieties you might meet. Black Willows grow to heights of 45 metres (148 feet) and have deeply furrowed grey bark when they get old. They're native to the whole eastern side of North America, from Arizona to Southern Ontario. You will find them growing at the edge of marshes, rivers, lakes and other areas with moisture in the ground.

Sandbar Willows are found in the sand and gravel bars of creeks and rivers. They are smaller than their cousins, the Black Willows, only growing as high as 7 metres (22 feet). The grey-green leaves of Sandbar Willows are very narrow and have irregular teeth. When these leaves are young, they have a smooth, soft white underside.

The Shining Willow takes its name from the Latin word *Lucida*, which means "to shine." And shine this Willow does! Its leaves are very glossy, and when the sun hits a patch of them they shimmer. This is a tall Willow, growing up to 15 metres (49 feet). When the trees are young, their bark is smooth with a deep golden colour.

Summer

The Latin word for Willow, *Salix*, means "to grow by the water." This is why I named my outdoor school Salix School. Just like Willows, kids are growing up near the water and are learning to be flexible.

Cool Facts about Willows

Willows are found all over the northern hemisphere, and their bendy branches have been used for centuries as a material for making baskets. Willow doesn't mind having some of its branches cut down; it just sprouts new ones. Basket makers do this by **coppicing** (cutting near the base of the tree) when they harvest branches, to keep young, straight branches forming every year. For many years, Willow has been used as medicine for headaches and pain and it's now made into the common drug called Aspirin.

Try This!

WILLOW CROWNS

Supplies needed:
- large Willow shoot
- hand pruners
- ribbon or string (optional)

Get to know the bendy quality of Willow by cutting a straight shoot as tall as yourself. This can be worked into a circular shape, weaving the ends together to form a crown. Collect other flowers, plants or feathers to weave into the crown. This might be a good thing to wear when using your magic wands (page 67) and saying the magic words of Latin names (page 125).

"I like Willows because you can often find birds' nests in them."
— Sophia, age 11

Look at the Willow crowns we made!

Willow 135

Viper's Bugloss

Echium vulgare L.

Harvesting Tip

The flowers on a Viper's Bugloss plant won't all be open at the same time. Pick them when they're open enough that you can see the bright-pink stamens.

Description

This little roadside plant easily captures the eye and the imagination. With its bristly leaves in a **basal rosette**, and **racemes** of vibrant purple-blue petals and neon-pink stamens erupting from a purple-spotted stem, Viper's Bugloss wins my award for coolest-looking weedy plant! It has a long and sturdy taproot, which means it's good at anchoring deep into soil. It's often found growing alongside other plants with taproots, like Queen Anne's Lace, Chicory and Mullein. These plants are important because they're often the only ones that can grow in the disturbed, compacted or unhealthy soil that occurs where people have built roads, strip malls or neighbourhoods.

Cool Facts about Viper's Bugloss

This plant got its funny, memorable name because people used to use it for snakebites. Like its cousin, Comfrey, Viper's Bugloss contains allantoin, a chemical that helps heal skin.

Try This!

VIPER'S BUGLOSS ICE CUBES

Viper's Bugloss flowers are edible, sweet and slightly gooey when chewed, just like the flowers of their cousin, Borage. Use them to add a bold pop of colour to salads or to decorate cupcakes. You can also freeze them into ice cubes to add a fun floral touch to summer iced tea or lemonade. Collect a small bowl of the open flowers. When you get home, place one flower in each section of an empty ice cube tray. Cover with water and place in the freezer for a few hours until frozen. When ready, pop out the cubes and enjoy them with your Wild Mint sun tea (page 110)!

Supplies needed:
- Viper's Bugloss flowers
- small bowl
- ice cube tray
- water

Check out this Hummingbird moth checking out the Viper's Bugloss!

Viper's Bugloss

Yarrow

Achillea millefolium

In Spain, archeologists found a 50,000-year-old Neanderthal skull with Yarrow still stuck in its teeth! Must have been a bad toothache.

Description

Yarrow is a perennial plant that grows about two feet tall. It starts out as a bunch of feathery, Fern-like leaves that are soft and smell sweet. In the late spring it sends up its woody stem, and in the summer it grows a crown of small white flowers. It might be hard to tell, but if you look up close, you can see that Yarrow is in the Aster family, even though its white umbels of flowers make it look like it's in the Carrot family.

Cool Facts about Yarrow

Yarrow is said to be the most widely recognized medicinal plant in the world. Not only that, it's one of the oldest plants to be used as medicine. Yarrow has many uses, but perhaps the one most useful to you will be for cuts. The Latin name for Yarrow, *Achillea*, is named for the Greek hero Achilles, who was said to have healed his warriors with Yarrow.

Summer

Try This!

YARROW FIRST AID

Yarrow is what is called a styptic, meaning it stops bleeding. When I teach knife skills to kids, I also teach them how to find Yarrow. If they cut themselves while carving, they know how to stop the bleeding.

Here is what you do:

"Ouch!" someone yells when their knife slips. Tell them to stay sitting down, hold on to the cut finger with their other hand

Chantel harvests Yarrow for first aid.

Yarrow 139

Margret uses Yarrow for first aid.

> **RED** stands for **R**est, **E**levate, **D**irect pressure.

and apply pressure, then raise it up. This is called RED, which stands for **R**est (stay sitting down), **E**levate (raise the injured part above the heart to slow the blood flow) and apply **D**irect pressure, which also slows the bleeding. Then ask someone who knows what Yarrow (or Plantain, which is also a styptic) looks like to gather a few leaves from a clean place nearby. Get the person with the cut to lightly chew up the leaves (but not swallow them) and then quickly let go of the cut and place the chewed-up leaves over top of it. Reapply the pressure, holding the leaves in place. After five minutes, have a look, and the bleeding will most likely have stopped. Then wash the cut with clean water and apply a bandage.

Note: This method is safe first aid for small superficial cuts, not deep gashes or anything that is bleeding a lot. If a cut hasn't slowed or stopped bleeding after five minutes, it may need stitches, and the hurt person should be taken to a clinic or emergency department.

Summer Scavenger Hunt

1. Collect three plants that can be used as medicine. Is there one that's good for cuts?
2. Find four examples of deciduous trees.
3. Collect three round stones: a white one, a black one and a green one.
4. Can you find any plants with edible fruit?
5. Find four plants that armour themselves with spikes, thorns, prickles or stingers.
6. Find one plant that likes to grow in moist soil and one plant that likes to grow in dry soil.
7. Collect three flowers. Look closely at them. How many petals do they have? Can you guess what family they're in?
8. Sit in a patch of shade. Which direction is the shade pointing?
9. Find three examples of a plant that has "gone to seed."
10. Collect three different types of grasses.

Summer flower scavenger hunt.

Yarrow

Autumn

Autumn usually begins golden and ends grey. Leaves of deciduous trees turn yellow, orange and red, then brown, and fall to the earth. Seeds are ripe and released to the ground, where they wait through winter to sprout in the spring. Late fruit is ripe and sweetens in the cold. The energy of the plants is down in their roots. This is a good time to harvest roots for food and medicine.

The colours of an Eastern autumn.

Chokecherry

Prunus virginiana

Description
Chokecherry grows as a large shrub or small tree in sunny open spaces. They're identifiable by their speckled bark and long, dangling clusters of creamy white flowers that are extremely fragrant (chokecherry is in the Rose family). Those blossoms turn into dark-red or purple fruits.

Cool Facts about Chokecherry
Chokecherries are incredibly sour and astringent in your mouth—so puckery that some people believe they make you choke, hence the name! But with added sugar, they're often cooked into sweet-tart jams and jellies. In the wild, they feed many species of animals, including bears, moose, coyotes, deer and birds who disperse the seeds widely. Indigenous people have also used the berries to help soothe diarrhea, sore throats and canker sores. Caution: Only the flesh of the fruit should be eaten; the seeds are toxic when consumed in large quantities.

The white clouds of Chokecherry blooms fill the spring air with sweetness.

Autumn 143

Ellianna looks at raccoon tracks.

Caution: Raccoon scat can have harmful parasites in it, so feel free to have a good look but do so with a stick so that you aren't breathing in the fumes! It might sound weird to look at something else's poop, but it's actually very cool; you can tell what the animal has eaten and where it has been.

Try This!

RACCOON TRACKING

In the fall, Chokecherry skins can be easily spotted in Raccoon **scat**. Raccoon tracks are easy to see in mud or the soft sand of a beach. Raccoons often like to have a poop on top of fallen logs. If you come across Raccoon scat with Chokecherry skins in it, look around and you'll probably find the tree not too far away. Raccoons like to walk on the side of creek beds where they can drink water and find yummy things like slugs. With five long toes, Raccoon tracks are very distinct and very cute. See how far you can follow the trail of the Raccoon. How long ago do you think it passed by? Can you tell how fresh the tracks are? How fresh is the scat? Can you see anything else in the scat that might tell you what the Raccoon has been eating? This activity can also be done in the city where Raccoons are happy to live and eat fruit like grapes, apples and raspberries from people's yards.

Chokecherry

The hand-like tracks of a Raccoon.

Elder

Red Elder
Sambucus racemosa ssp. *pubens*

Black Elder
Sambucus canadensis

Description

These deciduous shrubs like to live in moist forest clearings and along roadsides. Their long, pointy leaves grow opposite each other on the branch, and the shoots grow straight up. When Elder gets really old, its trunk and branches get gnarled and twisted. Red Elder flowers in May and sets its fruit midsummer, whereas Black Elder flowers in June, and its berries are ripe in September. The flowers are small white clusters that look like umbrellas. The berries form clumps of tiny round fruits of red or dark blue.

Cool Facts about Elder

All types of Elder were, and still are, eaten as an important food for Indigenous people of this region. Red Elderberries are always cooked; otherwise, they're poisonous. Many birds love to eat the berries as well, and you can often see flocks of Cedar Waxwings in these shrubs when the berries are ripe. The stems of Elder are filled with squishy pith and can easily be hollowed out. You can make beads by cutting the Elder stem crosswise into little rounds with a small saw. You can also cut a section as long as your hand to hollow out from one end as a straw or a place to put secret notes.

Autumn

Try This!

MAKE YOUR OWN ELDERBERRY SYRUP

Supplies needed:
- Black or Blue Elderberries
- picking bucket
- ladder (maybe)
- honey
- strainer or sieve

Picking off the berries to make Elderberry syrup.

> When I harvest Elderberries, I often stand on the roof of my truck to pick them. Breah thinks this is fun, but kind of embarrassing. It must be worth it, because once in a while she pretends to feel a bit sick, just for a sip of Elderberry syrup.

Black and Blue Elderberries have long been used as medicine. They're very high in vitamin C and are good for colds and flus. But the best part is that the syrup is so yummy, you can pour it on your pancakes! Collect Black Elderberries in the fall when they're ripe. They often grow up high on the branches, so you will need a ladder or a long rake to hook the branches down. Remember to leave some berries for the birds. Two cups will make enough syrup for the year. Rinse the berries when you get home, then put them in a heavy-bottomed saucepan. Cover them with twice as much honey and turn the pot on low heat on the stove. Let this simmer all day, without letting it come to a boil. When it's done, strain off the pulp from the berries and put the honey in a jar. This is your Elderberry syrup! You shouldn't need to keep it in the fridge but keep it somewhere cool and dark. The leftover berries that you strained off are delicious when made into tea—just pour boiling water over them, let them sit for ten minutes and drink!

Elder

Goldenrod

Solidago

Description

There are at least 100 species of Goldenrod, including more than 25 that are native to Ontario, so it can be tricky to distinguish one from one another. One of the most common varieties is Canada Goldenrod (*Solidago canadensis*), which blooms in loose, lanky clusters that look like plumes of bright-yellow feathers. Canada Goldenrod can spread by seed and rhizomes in a wide range of environments, including roadsides, disturbed soil and open fields and forests. More than 35 species of bees are specialist feeders on Goldenrod pollen, which means they only collect pollen from this plant! Goldenrod flowers late into the fall and provides important fuel for queen bumblebees preparing for winter and Monarch butterflies fuelling up to migrate.

Mullein

Verbascum thapsus

Description

Mullein likes to grow in **disturbed** soils. Look for the great, tall spires of yellow flowers on roadsides, cleared land, empty lots and dry, **arid** places. Mullein is a **biannual**, meaning it lives for two years. The first year it is a basal growth of soft, grey-green leaves, which sometimes grow bigger than your arm. In its second year, a flower stalk emerges, growing straight up, covered in soft, fuzzy leaves and ending in a spire of small yellow flowers. Some Mullein can grow up to 3 metres (9 feet) tall with multiple flower stalks that branch off, so that they look like the great Saguaro Cactus (*Carnegiea gigantea*) of the desert!

The leaves of the first year's growth can look similar to Foxglove, which is in the same family but is poisonous, so be sure to look closely before handling. Foxglove leaves are not as soft or thick as Mullein, nor do they have the same thick veins in the leaves. The leaves of Mullein grow in a basal form, whereas Foxglove leaves grow alternate.

This is a great plant to grow because it doesn't need any watering throughout dry summers, and it looks majestic in a garden.

Autumn

Making Mullein torches.

Harvesting Tip

Where Mullein grows, it's usually abundant enough to harvest with ease. If you are using the leaves to protect your feet from blisters or for hiker's toilet paper, just break the leaves off at the base. Mullein grows easily from seed, so if you want your very own Mullein patch, just collect some of the tiny black seeds at the end of summer and sprinkle them where you want them to grow. The seeds will sprout next spring and grow into big plants the year after. Bees will love the flowers!

Cool Facts about Mullein

Mullein was brought to North America with early settlers from Europe. It has long been used as medicine in both places. Like the softness of the leaves, it softens a sore throat or cough when drunk as a tea. Mullein has also been called Torch Plant, because the flower stalks were used as lanterns before people had electricity or even candles! The thick, soft leaves are great to stop blisters in your shoes and make a very nice "hiker's toilet paper." Caution: don't confuse Mullein with Foxglove or Comfrey when you use it for toilet paper. Trust me!

New England Aster

Symphyotrichum novae-angliae

Description

In late summer and early fall, this native plant bursts into hundreds of fuzzy-looking flowers that can range in colour from white (rarely) to pale-purple (most often) to deep-fuschia (occasionally). New England Asters are perennial and can grow up to 2 metres (around 6 feet) tall and around 1 metre (3 feet) wide. You can find these plants growing great clouds of purple petals in meadows, prairies, roadsides and city pollinator gardens too. New England Asters have composite flowers, which means each bloom looks like one single flower, but if you grab your magnifying glass and inspect one closely, you will see that it's actually made up of between one hundred and 150 teeny-tiny flowers. The yellow centre is a collection of tubular yellow florets that is surrounded by dozens of ray flowers, each one with a single lavender petal. At night, Asters close up, and all those miniscule flowers get folded into a package that opens again with the morning sun.

Autumn

The bees love the October New England Asters.

> The name Aster comes from the Latin word *Astrum*, which means "star." According to Greek mythology, the goddess Astraea looked at the earth and couldn't find any stars. She began to cry, and Asters sprouted wherever her tears soaked the ground.

Cool Facts about New England Aster

With hundreds of flowers that bloom in early autumn, each New England Aster is a pollinator power plant. Monarch butterflies feast on their nectar before making the long journey to Mexico for the winter, and their slender leaves are believed to feed caterpillars for over one hundred kinds of butterflies and moths. Their seeds also nourish the region's many songbirds, including Black-Capped Chickadees and American Goldfinches. New England Aster has been used in infusions to help treat diarrhea and fever as well as in smudges to help revive unconscious people.

Thistle

Canada Thistle
Cirsium arvense

Bull Thistle
Cirsium vulgare

Description
A Thistle is hard to miss, especially if you are walking barefoot through a field in summer! With their spiky leaves and bristly pink-to-purple flowers, they stand out in the grassy pastures, garden edges, roadsides and clearings where they like to grow. When they go to seed, their silky white fluff floats along and quickly spreads the seeds to grow new Thistles. Thistles are in the Aster family.

Cool Facts about Thistles
The Thistle is the emblem of Scotland. Some say the reason for this dates all the way back to the eighth century when the Norse army was invading Scotland. The Norse soldiers were sneaking up on the sleeping Scottish army when one of the Norse soldiers stepped on a Thistle and yelled so loud it woke up the sleeping Scots, who were then able to fight off the Norse.

Bull Thistle.

Autumn

Nibble This!

All Thistles are edible. We suggest wearing gloves when harvesting them to avoid the prickles, but if you don't have gloves, you can wrap a shirt or bandana around your hand. Use a digging stick to dig up the roots and include them in your wild root roast (page 156). Or cut the Thistle stem at the ground, use a rock to scrape off the spikes, then peel the stem and eat it like celery. The fleshy middle vein, or midrib, in the leaves can also be peeled and eaten. Use a rock to pound off the spikes on the leaves, then tear away the leaf, leaving just the midrib to eat.

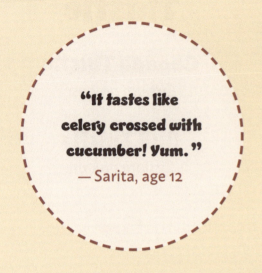

"It tastes like celery crossed with cucumber! Yum."
— Sarita, age 12

Preparing a Thistle leaf to eat.

Wild Carrot
(Queen Anne's Lace)
Dacus carrota

Description
Wild Carrot is also known as Queen Anne's Lace because its frilly, round umbels of flowers look like lace. In the centre of most of the flowers is one small dark-red flower, thought to be the blood of Queen Anne's head being chopped off. Yikes! This plant was introduced from Europe and is now found all over North America in open fields, meadows, roadsides and clearings. Before it flowers, its hairy leaves are long, green and feathery like a garden Carrot. The root of Wild Carrot is not orange, though; it is creamy white, long and narrow.

Autumn

Nibble This!

WILD ROOT ROAST

Supplies needed:
- digging stick or small shovel
- wild harvested roots
- a campfire or oven
- tin foil
- oven mitt
- salt and butter (optional)

There are so many wild foods to eat outside when you know where to look. This is a great autumn or winter activity for a fire on the beach. Using a digging stick (a stout stick about the size of two of your thumbs), gather the roots of Wild Carrot, Thistle and Dock. They're especially easy to dig in the sandy soils near a beach. Dust or wash the dirt off the roots, cut them into small pieces, then wrap them in three layers of tin foil. Add a diced potato if you like. Place the packages in the coals of a fire and let them roast for fifteen to twenty minutes, turning occasionally. Bring some salt along to sprinkle on them, or a bit of butter for a gourmet dining experience!

Mae harvests Wild Carrot root with a digging stick.

Harvesting Tip
. . . .

Caution: What plants are in the same family as Wild Carrot and are deadly poisonous? Poison Hemlock and Water Hemlock! So if you are harvesting Wild Carrot, please double check with a knowledgeable adult before touching the plant. Luckily, they grow in very different places: Water and Poison Hemlock grow at the edge of freshwater, and Wild Carrot prefers meadows, dry soil and road sides.

Above left: Wild Carrot and Indian Consumption plant roots for roasting.

Above right: Preparing wild roots to roast.

Wild Carrot   157

Wild Grape

Vitis vinifera ssp. *sylvestris*

Description

Wild Grapes are smaller, darker and much more sour than the grapes you find in the grocery store. They have abundant crunchy seeds and a bold flavour. You can nibble Wild Grapes when you see their beautiful purple clusters in the **understory** of many shrubs and trees, where they use their delicate but strong tendrils to climb around trunks and branches to reach for the sunlight. Wild Grape vines can grow as thick as a tree branch and become so tightly wound around trees that you can climb and swing on them (make sure you test their strength first). There are several species of Wild Grape that are abundant in the Northeast, and they can be used interchangeably for food and crafts. The most common one in Southern Ontario is the River Grape (*Vitis riparia*).

Cool Facts about Wild Grape

Charcoal made from burning the woody vines and twigs of Wild Grape makes a beautiful, rich black drawing material that artists have been using for centuries. You can also use them in recipes just as you would conventional grapes. Make your own wild jelly or jam or use the juice as a natural food colouring.

158   Autumn

Wild Grapes ready to snack on...
if you don't mind a sour crunch!

Harvesting Tip

To those unfamiliar with these plants, Wild Grape can bear a resemblance to its neighbour Virginia Creeper (*Parthenocissus quinquefolia*), another climbing vine with dark berries. Sometimes they like to grow near one another. But whereas Wild Grape has fruit dangling in dense clusters, Virginia Creeper has berries that are more spread out on bright-red stems. Get to know both plants before you harvest.

Wild Grape

Try This!

ARTISTS' CHARCOAL

Supplies needed:
- a piece of Wild Grapevine
- a tin with a tight-fitting metal lid (the kind used to store tea or biscuits)
- wood pruners
- tongs
- a campfire

Caution: Check the local campfire regulations before doing this activity.

Next time you have a campfire, search for Wild Grape. Using wood pruners, cut off a piece of vine that's as thick as an adult's finger and about 60 centimetres (2 feet) long. Then cut the vine into pieces about the same length (8 to 14 centimetres or 3 to 5 inches each). Place them in the tin and close the lid. With an adult's help, use tongs to insert the tin among the coals of your fire. You'll see smoke escaping from the lid of the tin. After about ten minutes, use tongs to carefully remove the tin. When the tin is cool enough to touch, remove your charcoal. You're ready to sketch!

Tip: You can use this technique to make charcoal out of any kind of stick. Willow charcoal is also traditionally used in art supplies. To make your own charcoal holder, gather pieces of pithy wood, like Elder or Sumac, and push out the soft pith with a nail, screwdriver or other tool. Then insert your charcoal.

Sketch the land with your Wild Grape charcoal.

160   Wild Grape

Autumn Scavenger Hunt

1. Collect five different types of deciduous leaves.
2. Arrange your leaves from red to green.
3. Find a plant that grows an edible root.
4. Can you find a plant that still has berries on it?
5. Find two plants that are native to the area and two plants that were introduced from Europe.
6. Can you find a tree that makes nuts or seeds?
7. Point to the south. This is the direction birds are headed on their migrations.
8. Find, but don't collect, one poisonous plant.
9. Look under a pile of leaves on the ground. Do you see any creatures?
10. Which deciduous tree has lost the most leaves?

What did Harriet find on this wet fall day? A shelter built with teamwork and deciduous leaves.

Enjoying autumn in the woods at nature school.

Wild Grape   161

Winter

The short days of winter are cold and snowy in the Great Lakes region. This is a time when plants rest or go **dormant**. Deciduous trees have lost their leaves. In late winter, when the days start to warm up but the nights are still cold, sap starts running in the trees. Reds and yellows come into the tips of the Willows, and we can see tiny buds forming on the end of the Maples, Roses and Wild Grapes. This is a great season for getting to know the evergreen trees in your area.

Balsam Fir

Abies balsamea

Description
These trees have flat needles with two white stripes. The needles grow straight out from either side of the twig. From a distance, the tree makes a very pointy cone shape. The bark of young trees is covered in sap blisters, and when the tree gets older, the grey bark gets furrowed. People often mistakenly call Fir cones pinecones, but unlike pinecones, which grow hanging down and drop to the ground, the cones of Balsam Fir stand up on their branches and don't drop to the ground. Once you see the difference, you will never call a Fir cone a pinecone again!

Winter

Amelie gets up close to a Balsam Fir.

Cool Facts about Balsam Fir

When Balsam Fir trees are young, the bark gets many sap bubbles under it, which kids love to pop and play with. This sap can be used to make glue. In May, when the Firs begin to grow for the year, the fresh tips are bright green. These are tasty and can be eaten fresh off the tree, added to salads or dried for tea. They're very high in vitamin C.

The wood of Fir trees can be full of sap or pitch. People will sometimes buy pitch wood at camping stores for lighting fires because the sap is so flammable. At Salix School, we often make our own pitch sticks for lighting campfires. With these, I have even been able to light a fire in a downpour!

> "I am so glad I brought my pitch wood!" Armas, age 9, said as he watched other kids struggling to light their own fires on the cold, rainy November day. With the help of his pitch wood his fire jumped to life. Soon, we all gathered around it.

One-Minute Mystery

I was walking through the forest one day when I spied something strange. There was a mushroom in a tree! Not growing out of the tree like a conk, but placed high up in the crook of a branch. As I looked around, I saw other mushrooms as well, placed higher than a human could reach, in the crook of a Fir branch. Who had put these mushrooms up there? After looking around a little more, I found a clue: a pile of scales from many Fir cones and a hole in the base of an old stump about as big as I could fit my arm in. Who dunnit?

ANSWER: Grey and Red squirrels like to collect mushrooms for their winter food. They're known for carrying them up a tree and placing them in the crook of a branch where the mushroom will dry and can be saved for a winter food source. Smart, hey? The pile of Fir cone scales was a squirrel midden, essentially the waste left behind after a squirrel has eaten the seeds from the Fir cones. The small hole was one of many openings to the squirrel's home.

We found Pine needles for our winter tea!

Balsam Fir **165**

Try This!

CAMPFIRE TEA

Supplies needed:
- fir tips
- metal kettle that can go on a fire
- small strainer
- non-breakable cups

Caution: Check the local campfire regulations before doing this activity.

Have you ever had tea made over a campfire? This is one of our nature school's winter highlights. Bring an old metal kettle (we call ours The Royal Kettle) especially for the occasion. Fill your kettle with water and bring it to a boil on the campfire. While waiting for the water to boil, ask an adult to tend the fire so you can collect some Fir tips, Pine needles or other tea plants. What wild tea ingredients do you think you might find on a cold December day? Use scissors to snip the Fir tips from the ends of a branch. When the water has boiled, have an adult take the kettle off the fire. Let the water cool just enough so it's no longer boiling; if it's too hot, it will draw out the plant's **tannins**, which taste yucky. Put the plants you gathered into your kettle or tea pot. Cover with a lid and let the tea steep for fifteen minutes. Be careful when you pour your tea because it will be hot! Strain and drink a warm cup of wild tea. Yum!

"*This is the best tea ever!*" — Bella, age 11, as she sipped her hot tea around our campfire. "*I think the Balsam Fir really makes it good.*"

Description

Hemlock has the shortest needles of all the evergreen trees in this region. It also has small cones. The needles form a dense, feathery pattern that doesn't let very much light pass through to the forest floor. This means not much grows under the Hemlock, except maybe more Hemlock, which doesn't mind growing in the shade. Hemlocks are easy to spot because the very top of the tree droops over to one side.

Cool Facts about Hemlock

Hemlocks have a lot of **tannins** in them. These make a reddish colour when the wood or branches are soaked in water. People use this to tan deer hides for making leather. The inner bark of Hemlock trees can be eaten like Pine.

Eastern Hemlock

Tsuga canadensis

Winter 167

Saving the Old-Growth Forest

Esme and Breah take a stand for their future.

I was nearing my eighteenth birthday when I learned of an old-growth forest that was due to be logged. A group of people had been trying to stop the ancient trees from being cut down, but the government and the logging company were not listening. I felt sad and angry that trees older than any human were being cut down to make lumber or, even worse, toilet paper. These forests were home to rare animals like the Northern Goshawk, a large, fierce raptor, and the Wolverine, an elusive, ferocious hunter in the weasel family. Didn't the government realize that we needed these old forests to help balance out the effects of the carbon emissions that cause climate change? Didn't they realize that these forests, with trees over 800 years old, are so rare that there are only 2 per cent of them left? Cutting them down is like killing Blue Whales! We realized that asking the government and the logging companies to stop cutting old-growth forests wasn't working. They didn't seem to care that it was our future, not theirs. All they cared about was making money.

So I got together with a group of friends, and we got ourselves organized. With people who knew what to do, we went to this beautiful forest and made it our home for a little while. We set up a kitchen and we built a few trails so that people could come and see how special these forests are. Sadly, the day the logging was to begin was fast approaching. All the talks and the marches in the city hadn't worked. By now, we had made friends with this old forest. We watched birds swoop between the branches. We swam in the cold river. We ate Blueberries until our fingers turned blue. What were we going to do? When you love something or someone, you can't stand and watch it get hurt.

After much thought, we decided we would move into the trees! Surely they couldn't cut the forest down if we lived in the trees! With climbing ropes and harnesses, platforms and pulleys, we made little houses way up high in the branches of the trees. I felt like a bird, way up there, 53 metres (175 feet) off the ground. As I lay cozy in my sleeping bag, I would watch as the sun made feathery shadows through the Hemlock branches. Pine Siskins would visit me for seeds from my trail mix. And for a while, the forest we loved was safe. No one could figure out how to get us down, and they couldn't cut the trees around us, because we might get hurt.

Then, on the morning of my eighteenth birthday, I heard a sound coming from the sky that wasn't a bird. It was a helicopter that had come to take us out of our trees. "Goodbye," I whispered to the feathery fronds of the Hemlock. "Goodbye," I called to Mouse who had stolen my peanuts so high up in the tree. Goodbye, beautiful old forest. I tried to save you, and that was the best I could do." I cried as I was taken away from my treetop home.

Eastern Hemlock

Eastern White Cedar

Thuja occidentalis

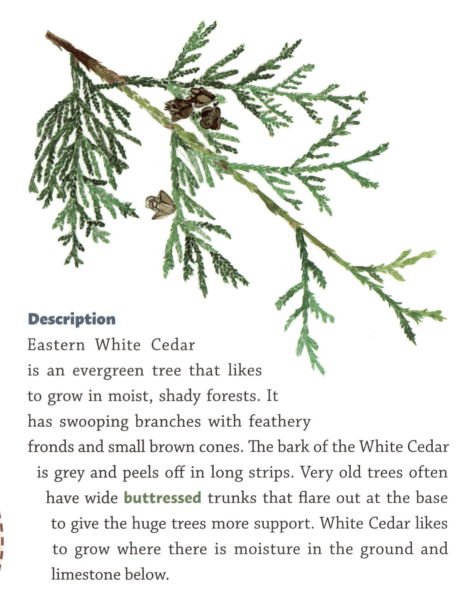

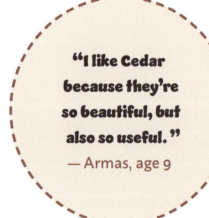

"I like Cedar because they're so beautiful, but also so useful."
— Armas, age 9

Description

Eastern White Cedar is an evergreen tree that likes to grow in moist, shady forests. It has swooping branches with feathery fronds and small brown cones. The bark of the White Cedar is grey and peels off in long strips. Very old trees often have wide **buttressed** trunks that flare out at the base to give the huge trees more support. White Cedar likes to grow where there is moisture in the ground and limestone below.

Cool Facts about Cedar

Even though the fronds of the Cedar are quite tough, White-Tailed Deer like to **browse** on them when there is little else to eat in the winter. In the days before stores, many useful items were made from Cedar, including clothes, blankets,

Winter

> If you are ever caught without soap after using the bathroom in the woods, you can rub your hands over the fronds of Cedar. The oils in Cedar are antiseptic like hand sanitizer. It's still a good idea to wash your hands well when you do find some soap and water.

Ian identifies Cedar in a Toronto park.

hats, containers, cradles, paddles, baskets, dishes, arrows, furniture, totem poles and medicine. The wood of Cedar is very rot-resistant, which makes it great for houses and canoes. In fact, it's so rot-resistant, that it can take a fallen Cedar up to 600 years to fully break down and turn back into the forest floor. Although these Cedars usually live until they're about 200 years old, some 700-year-old Cedars have been found growing in clefts between rocks in the Niagara Escarpment!

Eastern White Cedar.

Eastern White Cedar   171

Try This!

MAKE YOUR OWN TINDER

Supplies needed:
- strips of cedar bark
- knife or stone

The inner bark of Cedar makes great tinder, which, along with some pitch wood, will get a fire going in all weather. Find an older Cedar tree where some of the strips of bark are hanging a bit loose from the trunk. Notice what direction the wind and rain come from. Notice if one side of the tree is wet and the other dry. Now choose a dry place to pull off a strip of bark about as long as your forearm. The underside of the bark has a reddish-brown colour and is often dry. This red inner bark is what makes the tinder. With the edge of a stone or your knife, rub the soft inner bark off the thick outer grey bark. Then work the soft bark into smaller and smaller pieces until you have a fluffy pile of tinder. This can be put into your pocket to help dry it out even more until you light your fire. If you do this at the beginning of the day and have your fire in the afternoon, your tinder should be nice and dry. Remember, always ask an adult before you light a fire, and check the local rules about campfires.

Top left: Making tinder with the inner bark of Cedar.

Bottom left: Margret makes Cedar tinder.

Eastern White Pine

Pinus strobus

Description

There are at least five types of Pine that grow in the Great Lakes region, and Eastern White Pines have the longest needles, which grow in groups of five. You can see this when you look up close to the branch where the needles grow. Its pinecones are typically 8 to 20 centimetres long and look like what you think of when you hear "pinecone." White Pines usually grow tall and straight with an average height of 20 to 40 metres (65 to 131 feet), which makes them the tallest **conifer** to grow in this region. They're also one of the longest-living tree species in this part of the world, living around 400 years.

Cool Facts about Pine

The inner bark of Pine trees can be eaten. In fact, it's quite sweet, and the texture is a bit like chewing gum crossed with noodles. The sap is also sweet and can be collected to cook down into glue for sealing boats and making tools. The sap helps heal cuts just by putting it right on the wound.

> "When I find a ball of pine sap, I like to chew it like chewing gum!"
> — Tosh, age 12

Winter

Try This!

PINECONE BIRD FEEDERS

Supplies needed:
- large pinecones
- peanut butter or lard
- bird seed
- a tray or baking sheet
- string

Many birds like to eat the seeds from inside pinecones. Now you can give them another treat. Once the cones fall to the ground, the birds are usually done with them. Collect a few cones. Tie a string around one end. Then you can roll the cones in either peanut butter or lard, or use a butter knife to smear it on and under the scales. On a tray or baking sheet, pour out some bird seed and then roll your sticky cone in the bird seed, shaking off the extra when you are done. Hang these in the trees of your yard so you can enjoy the feeding flocks of winter Juncos, Nuthatches, Chickadees and Pine Siskins.

Who will come eat the seeds at this Pine cone bird feeder?

Eastern White Pine 175

Maple

Sugar Maple
Acer saccharum

Black Maple
Acer nigrum

Norway Maple
Acer platanoides

Black Maple.

Description
There are over ten different types of Maples found in this region. The most famous one is the Sugar Maple, whose sap has the highest concentration of sugars in it, making it great for syrup. The **palmate** leaves of Sugar Maple usually have five lobes and three main veins. They grow opposite from each other on stems that are about the same length as the leaves off the branch. Sugar Maples can live to be up to 400 years old! Black Maples are very similar to Sugar Maples, but their leaves only have three lobes, and they droop instead of sticking straight out like Sugar Maple leaves do. Norway Maples were introduced to the region from Europe in the mid-1700s as a shade tree. (Were there not any other trees here then?) Unlike the native Maples' thick rough bark, Norway Maple has smooth bark. These trees are brittle, and the branches break easily. These leaves ooze milky sap when you break them.

Cool Facts about Maple
In the spring, the blossoms of Maples are abuzz with the sound of bees. These bright flowers are edible and are best eaten before they're fully open. You can pop them into your mouth as a snack or harvest some to steam like broccoli or add to a quiche. The helicopter seeds, called samaras, are great fun to throw up into the air and watch twirl down to the ground. The seeds sprout easily and can be transplanted to a garden or an area in need of trees.

Try This!

MAKE YOUR OWN MAPLE SYRUP

Supplies needed:
- middle-aged Sugar Maple tree
- clean bucket
- hammer and 3" nail
- drill with ½" to 1" bit
- spigot or clean ½" to 1" piping
- large pot
- wood stove, campfire, camp stove or home stove

Do you like Maple syrup? I sure do! Although Sugar Maples have the highest concentration of sugar in their sap, delicious syrup can be made by collecting sap from any kind of Maple. Gathering the sap is best done in late winter when the nights are cold—below freezing—and the days are just above freezing. This ensures that the sap will be running up and down the tree. You will need to buy some spigots, which you can find online or at your local hardware store. You can also make some by bending aluminum pie plates into little tubes. With the help of an adult, drill a hole about a half an inch wide into the trunk of a mid-sized tree whose bark is not yet thick like that of an old tree. The hole will not hurt the tree. Insert your spigot into the hole. Hammer a nail below the hole on which to hang a clean bucket in the evening. When the sap is running freely, check

Stella and Tom check the Maple sap bucket.

Maple 177

Never too cool to eat Maple blossoms!

In Japanese, the word *momijigari* means "maple leaf hunting," and is an activity that people still do today. This autumn, go out and do your own *momijigari* by finding as many beautiful leaves as you can!

your bucket midday to see how much Maple sap you have gathered. This Maple water is delicious to drink fresh from the tree.

To make it into syrup, the sap needs to be boiled down. The best way to do this is to put it in a stainless steel pot on top of your wood stove if you have one. Otherwise, you can do it on your kitchen stove (with the fan going), a camp stove outside or by hanging it over an open fire outside. Turning the Maple water into syrup takes patience. The heat helps the water evaporate, leaving the sugars behind in the pot. Depending on how much sap you're boiling, it can take a few hours. Be sure to keep your eye on it so it does not burn. It takes anywhere between 20 to 100 litres (around 5 to 26 gallons) of sap to make 100 millilitres (less than half a cup) of syrup…but it's worth it!

"We made snow taffy with our Maple syrup, and it was the most delicious thing I had ever tasted."
— Stella, age 7

Description

Usnea is a **lichen** that looks like long strands of hair. It is pale grey-green and has a rough texture. There are other similar-looking lichens. To tell them apart, gently pull on a strand of *Usnea*. There you will find a stretchy cord in the middle. *Usnea* grows draped from the branches of old trees.

Usnea.

Old Man's Beard

Blood-Spattered Beard (!)
Usnea wirthii

Methuselah's Beard
Usnea longissima

(I just call it *Usnea*.)

Cool facts about *Usnea*

Usnea only grows in healthy forests. When you see *Usnea* on trees, you know that the air of the forest is clean and that the forest is old. *Usnea* used to be widespread in northern forests, but there are now many places where it doesn't grow because of air pollution or logging. *Usnea* is a lichen, and a lichen is like two creatures in one. It's part fungi, which means "mushroom," and part **algae**. The fungi make a thick armour to protect the algae on the inside. The algae's job is to use the sun for photosynthesis. *Usnea* is used as a very strong medicine for colds and flus, infections and lung problems.

Winter 179

Hey, you aren't an old man—
but nice Old Man's Beard!

Try This!

HEALTHY FOREST INQUIRY

Have you walked in a forest where *Usnea* grows? What did it feel like? Have you walked in forests where there is no *Usnea*? How were these forests different? What does a forest need to be healthy?

I once had a woman come to me with an infected spider bite. She had gone to a few doctors and even taken antibiotics, but none of them cured the infection. I showed her how to make tea from the *Usnea*. She used it as a wash and as a drink, and within a week her infection had healed up!

Harvesting Tip

Never pick *Usnea* off a tree where it's growing, as it takes a long time to grow. The best time to gather *Usnea* is after a big windstorm, when it is blown down out of the trees. It will dry easily in a basket and can be kept for tea in a bag or jar. This tea can be used for colds, flus, and as a powerful wash for healing Brown Recluse spider bites. I use *Usnea* medicine to help people heal from respiratory infections, so I go out walking after storms to gather it.

Cougar Tracking

Caution: Even though this is an exciting story, it should not be tried at home. Cougars can and do attack people. I share it here to show the relationship between plants, the land and animals.

It was late winter, and the snow had begun to melt, leaving patches of bright-green moss sticking up like islands through the snow. My fourteen-year-old nephew, Raph, and I were on the trail of a Cougar. Or so we thought. Or maybe hoped. There had been reports (or rumours) of Cougar sightings in the area. Winter is often the time they come to feast on the overabundance of White-Tailed Deer who live here.

One of our neighbours had reported looking out her kitchen window right into the eyes of a female Cougar while she was in the middle of making dinner! We had to see for ourselves. Cougars are dangerous animals, so we didn't actually want to get up close and personal with one, but we wanted to see its tracks in the snow. We wanted the thrill of standing right where a Cougar had stood. Knowing that cougars stay on the move, we knew we probably wouldn't actually get to see it. Soon enough, though, we found her tracks. They were the size of my hand! In the melting snow they were hard to follow, but we pieced together the Cougar's trail across the road, through the woods and across a mossy bluff. There, at the top of the bluff, was a big Cougar scat, plopped right on a clump of blown-down *Usnea*, with some hasty scratches of dirt on top. Like house cats, cougars always cover their poop.

If you see fresh Cougar tracks in the snow, it's not a good idea to follow them back to the Cougar!

From there, a rough trail slid down the face of the ridge to an overhang of rock. Below, it was the perfect place for a Cougar to sleep. Sure enough, there were a few hairs on the dirt floor. I put my hand down on the bed where the Cougar had slept. It was still warm! The hairs on the back of my neck stood up, and my knees shook.

"Raph," I said to my nephew, "I think we should get out of here."

"Yes," agreed Raph, "But don't run; cougars like to chase people."

We carefully made our way down the rest of the ridge. There, at the bottom, as if to confirm all our hopes (and fears!) was the carcass of a dead deer. It looked as if an animal had recently been eating it.

"Yikes!" yelled Raph. "Run!"

"But you said not to!" I called, even as I began to run.

"Well, do it anyway!" Raph yelled as we headed up the trail.

And we did, all the way home, stopping only briefly to point out a second dead deer, just down the path from the front door.

182   Old Man's Beard

Red Oak

Quercus rubra

Description

These are fast growing Oaks and can reach up to 6 metres (20 feet) in just ten years. In spring, summer and fall they're easy to recognize by their pointy leaves, but in the winter, when they lose their leaves, you need to get up close to know them. Have a look at their bark and you will see that the ridges running all the way up and down the trunk have deep-red stripes. This is the only type of Oak with this marking.

Cool Facts about Red Oak

This tree is native to eastern North America and was introduced to Europe in the 1700s as a source of fast-growing wood. It's now considered one of the most invasive trees in Europe. (Often the opposite is true: plants native to Europe were brought to North America.)

For the acorns of this tree to germinate, they need to be exposed to cold 4°C (40°F) for at least three months. With changes in the climate, some years no Red Oak acorns

---

One of the oldest trees in the city of Toronto is the Zhelevo Red Oak, at 250 years old. You can go see it in North York. The circumference of its trunk is nearly 5 metres (over 16 feet)! How many people do you think it takes to hold hands around its trunk?

Winter 183

> The acorns of the Red Oak are very bitter, but mice and deer don't care and are happy to eat them as nutritious winter food.

will sprout because they don't get enough cold. Like most deciduous Oak trees, Red Oak starts leafing out and sending out its catkins when there are thirteen hours of daylight in the spring. The tree only cares how light it is, not how cold it is. This means that sometimes Oaks will put out their leaves and flowers, only to have a cold frost kill them, which prevents acorns from sprouting that year. When the days shorten in the fall, to eleven hours, this is the signal for the Oak to drop its leaves.

Right: An old Red Oak tree, older than you or me, growing in the open edge of a farm field.

Try This!

NATURE CLOCK

Supplies needed:
- a straight stick
- several small to medium stones

Tell time with a stick and stones.

Like the Red Oak who knows when to sprout or drop its leaves depending on the amount of daylight, we can also keep track of time by watching the world around us. On a sunny day, you can make a simple sundial. Find a straight stick about 60 centimetres (2 feet) long and a collection of small to medium stones. Choose a sunny spot and press the stick into the ground with a slight slant to the north. Notice what time it is and where the shadow of the stick is pointing. Place the corresponding number of stones to the hour at the shadow's edge (one stone for one o'clock, two stones for two o'clock). Every hour, go to your sundial and place the next number of stones at the end of the shadow. At the end of the day, you will have a semi-circle of stones that will tell you the time. Notice at which pile of stones the shadow falls when it is lunchtime, when you play tag, when you go home for the day or any other time you want to mark. Place an object such as a pinecone, cool leaf or flower at each of these places. When you come back the next day, you can use this clock to tell the time. "The shadow is pointing at the Oak leaf, so it's snack time!"

> "I was sure that the Maple twig was a Beech twig until I remembered that Maple buds are opposite each other and Beech are alternate. Once you figure out the patterns, it's so much easier to tell the difference!"
> — Alexander, age 9

Try This!

GUESS THIS BUD

Winter is a great time to practice your plant identification skills. During the rest of the year there are leaves or flowers to give you clues as to what plant you are looking at. In winter, we have an extra challenge telling who is who without these. Choose three to five twigs from various deciduous trees. Look closely at each one. What do the buds look like? Do they have catkins? What pattern is the bark? Do the buds smell or are they sticky? Give them to your friend, parent or instructor and have them guess which twig belongs to which tree. Now it's your turn: can you guess three or four twigs given to you? Once you do this a few times, you will never mix up Beech with Oak or Aspen again!

Guess the twig!

Red Oak

Try This!
. . . .

WHO AM I?

Write out the names of local plants on pieces of masking tape, enough so that every person gets at least one. For the advanced version, use Latin names. Each person gets a piece of tape with a plant name stuck to their forehead without them seeing what is written on it. Using yes-or-no questions, have the players try to find out which plant they are. For example: "Am I a tree with needles? Do I have small cones? Do I like to grow in sunny places?" This is a great way for players to identify and get to know plants while also building the skill of asking questions.

Supplies needed:
- masking tape
- pen
- four to twenty players

Isabella and Breah playing the "Who am I?" game.

Red Oak

A winter scavenger hunt in a city park.

Winter Scavenger Hunt

1. Find three plants with thick or waxy leaves. Why do you think they grow like this?
2. Find four examples of something that is growing but is not technically a plant.
3. Collect three different types of evergreen cones.
4. Collect a part from three plants that have died back for the winter.
5. Can you find the tracks of an animal?
6. Listen quietly. Can you hear any birds? What are they eating?
7. Can you find any clues to tell how much snow has fallen in the last week?
8. Find two types of plant or tree material that could be used for dry tinder or fire starter.
9. Can you see any examples of an animal eating plants or cones?
10. Find one plant that you can eat at this time of year.

Tree Quiz

1. What tree makes clothes, medicine, houses, canoes, tools and baskets?
2. Is a Maple tree deciduous? How about a Pine tree? What about a Spruce?
3. True or false: Spruce trees make large cones.
4. How do you know when you are shaking hands with a Spruce tree?
5. Which of these trees has needles: White Pine or White Cedar?
6. Name two trees that make catkins. What are catkins?
7. True or false: Oak leaves are "toothed."
8. Which tree makes acorns and provides important food for animals?

Which type of Pine do we have here?

ANSWERS: 1. Cedar. 2. Yes, no, no. 3. False. 4. The needles are sharp. 5. White Pine. 6. Oak and Cottonwood have catkins, which are hanging strands of small flowers. 7. True. 8. White Oak

9

For Parents and Educators

We have all the statistics we need about children spending less time outside and too much time inside on screens. Most of us know, even intuitively, that our kids need fresh air to flourish. Despite this, many parents and educators struggle with how to shift this balance.

My suggestion is to start close to home. If you live in the city, find a park, empty lot or backyard to become your place of connection to nature. Plants are everywhere. So are birds,

insects and animals. Many people tell themselves that they can't connect to nature unless they're in the "wilderness," but this doesn't need to be true. A Blue Jay calls from the telephone wire, just as a Chickadee calls from a Chokecherry Tree. A Cooper's Hawk is just as likely to swoop down and catch either bird by surprise. Raccoons cross my rural yard just as they will cross the sidewalk in front of a city house. Dandelions grow on lawns and in backyards all over the northern hemisphere. It matters less where you get outside than that you are getting outside. (That said, if you have the means, make sure you and your family experience the wonder of an old-growth forest before they're gone.)

Wilderness connection and outdoor activities are dominated by white, middle-class, able-bodied people, like me. While holding the awareness that not everyone has the time, energy, money or capacity to go into the wilderness, I encourage everyone to get outside in some way. You don't need fancy gear, or even a car. Find a park in your neighbourhood that is accessible. Join a group of families who go out together. Support each other by sharing rides, gear, ideas and kid care. Let's work together to break down the race and class barriers that separate people from each other and from the world of the outdoors.

The future of this planet and all the species that live here depends on today's children connecting to where they live and the other living beings there. Becoming attuned to nature and to one's senses brings higher levels of empathy, nourishes the nervous system, and increases a feeling of

Telling stories around the autumn fire.

connectedness rather than separation. These are qualities that encourage communication, community, self-confidence, trust and leadership. When a child, or an adult, has a relationship with a place and the creatures who live there, whether it is an abandoned lot, their backyard or an ancient rainforest, they care for it and become its stewards.

In this time of climate chaos, social upheaval, class and racial division and increasing addiction to screens, reconnecting to nature is a high priority. My hope with this field guide is that through hands-on activities, children and adults alike will be able to go beyond just naming a plant or tree to developing a relationship with it. By eating, drinking and using materials from the world around us, we engage in reciprocity and experience the generosity of the earth. This in turn helps us feel at home in the outdoors, reminding us that the earth has always provided us with all our basic needs and that we must care for the earth in return.

This field guide is for children, youth and adults. Although I have included some technical language as a way of introducing the vocabulary of botany into our daily lives, most of the book is written to be accessible and interesting to people of all ages. Once again, it's the relationship with place and plants that has the impact, not whether a person can tell the difference between petals or bracts. With enough time, the science and the intuition merge to create a holistic way of knowing a plant.

Tips for Adults

Teaching nature connection to children is a bit of a misnomer. Without our meddling, children are inherently connected to nature. It is only through socialization that they become disconnected from nature. Perhaps we need a guide not on nature connection but on "how to not disconnect from nature in the first place"! Keeping this in mind, here are some ideas for how to encourage deeper connection with the outdoors.

Playing bat and moth.

Whose feather is this?

- Being outside is fun! Children need to be in their bodies, to move and to be in a state of wonder and play. If they're out of this habit, it may take some convincing and some modelling to help them remember how to play. Run, play tag, build faerie houses or forts, listen to the birds and get dirty. Join them in the fun.
- Have a regular, built-in practice in your home or classroom life that gives children unstructured time in unstructured places where spontaneous interactions with imagination, plants and creatures can happen.
- Model play, inquiry and connection. When outside with kids, engage. Find things that pique your interest and share your enthusiasm. Look up things you don't know online or in field guides with the kids. Ask children what they think, what they notice, what surprises them.
- Asking questions rather than giving answers encourages deeper learning. When children have to find answers themselves, they will feel connected to the process of inquiry. Groups of children love the challenge of solving a problem together. Give them challenges that make them think beyond a surface answer.
- Interact with your surroundings. Show them that it's okay to get dirty digging up roots. Crouch down to look closely at a flower. Munch some Miner's Lettuce. Collect some leaves. Be part of the world, because you are.

Even with the warmth of a campfire, kids need many layers of winter clothes to stay warm and happy outdoors.

Tools, Supplies and Safety

One of the great parts of connecting with nature is that you don't need anything except yourself to do it. Your eyes, ears, hands, feet, mouth and heart are all the equipment you need. That said, there are a few things that can help further your connection and interaction with the world of plants. Here are some items I recommend and some supplies you will need to do some of the activities in this book.

Outdoor Gear

Quality winter gear allows everyone to be comfortable outside. Choose boots and jackets that are easy to move around in and equally warm and waterproof. During the rainy season, choose boots that keep your feet dry, while still allowing for climbing and running. A lot of rain gear these days does not actually keep a person dry, and being wet and cold is

Chapter 9

much worse than just being cold. Good gear is costly, and we don't all have the funds for it. Check out used gear swaps. Many communities are starting libraries where you can borrow outdoor gear. Check to see if your community has one. If not, start one.

Knives

Kids love the agency of having their own knife. In my outdoor program, I start most kids with their own knife and teach them knife skills at age five, give or take. But not all kids. I have to see that they're ready. Some signs of knife readiness include:
- able to follow directions
- able to sit still
- able to do other projects, like crafts, that require manual dexterity and hand-eye coordination
- an interest in knife-associated skills, such as food preparation or whittling

At the nature school where I teach, I suggest fixed-blade knives like Mora knives, which have a well-fitted sheath. These are good for bushcraft applications like splitting pitch wood and cutting thick- or woody-stemmed plants. A folding

Making a feather stick.

Opinel knife.

knife with an easy lock, like an Opinel, is also a good choice because it fits small hands and has a sensitive blade for carving and cutting food. Both of these knives are easy to handle, safe, and lend themselves to being sharpened. Stay away from folding knives with no lock like Swiss Army knives. Blades should be no more than 10 centimetres (4 inches) long. A knife is less likely to cut the user if it is well sharpened, which is a skill I teach once other basic knife skills are met.

To begin teaching knife skills, I sit with the child one-on-one at first, demonstrating basic whittling, cutting away from themselves and determining which wood to choose. When I see safe knife use, children are allowed to use their knives in groups at carving time or activities where knives are appropriate. All children must ask before they take out their knives and only when they're sitting down with a "blood bubble" around them. The blood bubble is a key to knife safety. This means checking with the knife user's outstretched arms that the area around them is safe and there is no one else in the blood bubble. The knife must always be put away properly before the child stands up.

When a knife user accidentally cuts themself for the first time, I celebrate the consequence of tool use, clean and treat the cut with Yarrow or Plantain, apply a bandage and encourage the child to continue. Most knife cuts that happen when a child is learning to use a knife are minimal and safe if the knife is being used properly.

Chapter 9   **197**

June learning carving.

Other Sharp Tools

Small folding saws, light hatchets and hand pruners are useful tools for cutting staves, making kindling, cutting branches, snipping up roots for medicine and cutting saplings for structures. These are tools reserved for skilled hands; although some six-year-olds can use these tools with proper instruction and supervision, the tools are more often in the hands of a teenager or adult. Any age is a great age to teach the empowerment that comes with tool use.

Matches, Lighters, Glint and Steel and Ferro Rods

Not everyone lives in a place where making a fire outside is an option. For some people, sitting around a campfire is a once-in-a-lifetime experience that is remembered fondly. Making tea from wild plants over a fire is one of my favourite activities to do in the winter. Find out what parks, beaches or recreation sites near you allow outdoor fires and when the local fire bans are, so that you can share the wonderful experience of a campfire with kids!

There are many ways of lighting a fire when you are outside. I find the easiest method for children is with good-quality wooden matches, as long as a fire is well built with dry tinder. Lighters are challenging, because they get hot and have a tendency to burn the thumb. A flint and steel or ferro rod takes practice, but a fire lit with a spark from these is exciting. Small, fluffy, dry tinder is a must!

Good-quality matches help kids practice fire-starting skills.

When working with fire, tie back long hair, roll up sleeves and remove puffy jackets. Children at my outdoor school are challenged to build their own fires but have to ask before they take out any matches or lighters. I encourage them to use as few matches as possible by handing out the matches instead of giving them the whole box. This ensures they're mastering their fire-making skills and not using the matches as tinder! Before they try lighting the fire, check that they're safe and that they have the proper materials at hand: dry tinder, small twigs, mid-sized pieces of wood as well as larger ones. "A fire is like a hungry baby," I tell them, "it wants to be fed a lot of small bites."

Chapter 9   **199**

Poet makes a map.

Pen, Paper, Sketchbooks and Art Supplies

Drawing plants while actually sitting right next to them is an irreplaceable way to really see a plant. Not only might the artist see parts of the plant they never noticed before, but they can convey the "feeling" of a plant even if the drawing does not botanically represent the plant. Providing the artists with their own sketchbooks and quality art supplies like pencils, pencil crayons, pastels and felt-tip markers enhances the experience. A small pocket-sized notebook is helpful for jotting down questions, observations, mysteries and leaf and plant sketches to look up later.

Magnifying Glass and Jewellers' Loupe

Jewellers' loupes, which fold up into a small case, can be easily carried on a cord around the neck, while magnifying glasses are a little bulkier. Both are great for bringing the world of the small into focus. Pollen anthers, iridescent beetle shells, leaf edges, feathers and millions of other finds become a whole new experience when seen up close.

Medicine-Making Supplies

Small clean jars with tight-fitting lids can be kept out of the recycling, or you can purchase small canning jars. Baby food jars and washed skin cream jars can be reused for salves and oils.

Use organic or extra-virgin cold-pressed oils (make sure that they're not rancid).

Beeswax can be purchased from local beekeepers or craft stores. You can also use the ends of old candles, as long as they're 100 percent beeswax. Give them a little rinse first.

If you are adding essential oils to your salve, make sure they're pure essential oils, not "fragrances," which are often synthetic. Always label everything you make. You might think you will remember, but even after all these years, I still have to compost something every now and again that I did not label because I forgot what it was. I like to use green painters' masking tape because it's easy to remove once I'm done.

Small jars, beeswax and measuring cups are useful medicine-making supplies.

Chapter 9   **201**

Glossary

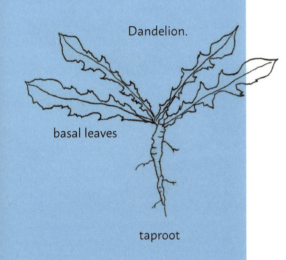
Dandelion.
basal leaves
taproot

algae: plant-like organisms that contain chlorophyll but do not flower

alkaloid: naturally occurring chemicals in plants

arid: dry

basal: growing from the base of the plant or stalk

basal rosette: leaves growing all around the base of the stalk of a plant

biannual: a plant that flowers in its second year

bog: a low wet area

botanist: someone who studies plants

bracts: a leaf of a tree or plant that looks like a petal

broad-leaved: a deciduous tree

browse: to nibble the twigs, shoots, leaves and berries of shrubs

buttress: a wide base that flares out to support trees or buildings

carnivore/carnivorous: a plant or animal who eats other creatures

catkins: the long dangling groups of small flowers on trees like Hazel or Alder

clan: a subclass of a plant family (e.g. the *Rubus* clan)

compostable: a natural material that will break down into tiny particles and turn back into the earth

conifer/coniferous: a tree or forest of trees that have needles or fronds, not leaves (e.g. Balsam Fir)

convulsions: extreme shaking

coppicing: a traditional method of harvesting wood without killing a tree

corm: an underground stem that stores nutrients for the plant

deciduous: a tree or herbaceous plant that loses its leaves in the autumn

dioecious: female reproductive parts and male reproductive parts (flowers) on separate plants

disturbed: ground that has been changed from its original state by fire, road building, machinery or grazing

dormant: when a plant is not growing, often in winter or during a drought

ecosystem: an interaction between land, water, animals and plants that forms an interdependent community

ecology: the study of the relationships between plants, their environment and each other; the specific place animals or plants live

elaiosome: a fleshy part attached to a seed that attracts ants to help with seed dispersal

emetic: something that makes you throw up

ephemeral: plants that have a short life span or are only above ground for a short time

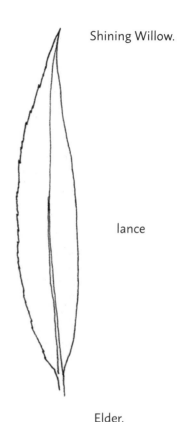

Shining Willow.

lance

Elder.

opposite

Maple.

lobe

palmate

Plantain.

parallel veins

ethical: something done with respect and care

evergreen: a tree or plant that stays green all year, either with needles or leaves

fertile: able to make new plants

freshwater: found in lakes, rivers and ice, as opposed to salt water found in oceans and seas

frond: a large divided leaf, like that of a Fern or Cedar tree

fungi: the scientific word for mushrooms

genocide: the intentional destruction of a racial or cultural group

habitat: a specific place that an animal or plant needs to live

hardwood forest: the main type of forest in the Great Lakes region, consisting mostly of deciduous trees, including Sugar Maples

herbicides: chemicals that are sprayed on plants to control their growth or kill them

Indigenous: people who have lived in a place since Time Immemorial, long before settlers came from elsewhere; plants or animals who originated in an area

invasive plants: plants that come from a different area and take over the habitat of other plants

lance-shaped: leaves shaped like a spear tip or knife

laxative: something that makes you poop

lichen: an organism that is made up of both algae and fungi

lobed: a leaf with round, bumpy edges

monoculture: the practice of growing only one kind of crop or raising one kind of animal on a farm

204 Glossary

mycelium: the underground root-like parts of fungi that feed it and connect and communicate with the forest

myrmecochorous: seed dispersal by ants

nervous system: the part of your body in charge of all the movements you don't think about, like breathing and heart beats; also in charge of how you sleep and respond to stress

node: place where a leaf or stems attaches or grows from

northern hemisphere: the part of the earth that is north of the equator

old-growth forest: a forest of very old trees that has never been logged

opposite: leaves that grow across from each other on the same stem

parallel veins: veins of a leaf that run straight next to one another

palmate: leaves like the shape of a palm of a hand (e.g. Maple)

parasite: an animal or plant who lives off another animal or plant, often harming their host

perennial: a plant that lives for more than two years

pesticides: chemicals that are sprayed on insects to kill them

photosynthesis: the chemical process plants use to turn sunlight into food

pollinator: an insect or animal that carries pollen from one flower to another

pollinating: when pollen from a female part of a plant mixes with the pollen from the male part of a plant to produce fertile seed, which can then grow more plants

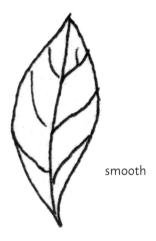

Blueberry.

smooth

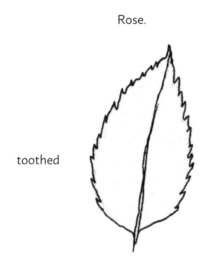

Rose.

toothed

racemes: a long cluster of flowers that opens from the twig end

rhizome: a root that travels underground with nodes that can sprout into new shoots of the plant

runners: like a rhizome but at the surface of the soil; a way for a plant to spread along the ground

scat: animal poop

sepals: the outer petal-like covering of the petals, often green under the petals

spadix: the floral spike found within the spathe

spathe: bract-like cover over the spadix, found on plants like Skunk Cabbage

species: a way of organizing types of living creatures into groups

spores: the tiny cells that ferns, lichens and mosses use to reproduce

stamen: the part of the flower that produces pollen

sterile: not able to reproduce or make new plants

stratification: the process of exposing seeds to cold to allow them to germinate

styptic: a plant that stops bleeding

subclass: a smaller group of plants with shared characteristics within a plant family

tannins: a reddish coloured natural chemical found in some plants like Oak and Hemlock; used to make dyes

umbels: umbrella-shaped flowers

understory: the plants that make up the forest beneath the trees

veins: the part in a leaf that moves water and food, often visible as lines in the leaf

volatile oils: natural chemicals in plants that have a strong smell and can be used as medicine

watershed: a river system that all higher water drains into

wildcrafting: harvesting plants for food or medicine in the wild

wildlife tree: old trees with holes in them that animals use for homes or food sources

Acknowledgements

My deepest gratitude goes to the plants themselves and the lands, waters and animals that nourish them. Without these, nothing would be. Thank you to Danielle Hagel, who shared her knowledge and love of the plants of the Great Lakes region. I am hugely grateful to all those who work to keep our world healthy: the land, water and animal protectors and defenders, those on the front lines and those in the background. Thank you to those who keep stories, knowledge and tradition alive: the Elders of this place, the Indigenous people of the past and present whose long relationship with the land and plants has created such beauty and generosity. I feel deep respect for those who are working to restore and encourage culture and connection with the land. Without all this work, without all the stories and teachings handed down, we would have very little of this knowledge. I am grateful to the ancestors of this land, the people of this land and the descendants of this land for having me here. I acknowledge the loss and trauma that occurred on this land that has allowed me and other non-Indigenous people to make our homes here. Thank you to the K'ómoks, Pentlatch, Qualicum, Homalco, Klahoose, Tla'amin, We Wai Kai and We Wai Kum people of central "Vancouver Island" whose lands I live on now. Thank you to the Lekwungen, W̱SÁNEĆ, Musqueam, Squamish and Tsleil-waututh people whose lands I have lived on in the past. These lands, waters and plants have nourished me and my family.

I have had many human teachers as well and I thank them, especially Jasmyn Clift, Mimi Kamp and Nadine Ijaz. Some of my other human teachers are the kids I spend my days with at our outdoor school called Salix School on Sla-Dia-ach, or Denman Island, where I live. "Salix" is the Latin name for Willow, which, like the kids, grows near water and is resilient and flexible. I learn so much through the wonderful curiosity, keen attention and endless questions of children.

Thank you to all the kids who have learned about this beautiful world with me, and to the ones who are in the photos: AC, Akai, Alexander, Amelie, Arawyn, Astrid, Astrud, Avery, Bella, Breah, Briar, Chantel, Chantel #2, Elli, Gabby, Harriet, Ian, Isabella, June, Liam, Louisena, Mae, Margret, Maya, Milliano, Naomi, Naya, Poet, Raphael, Rueben, Sarita, Sophia, Stella, Taya and the other Taya, Tosh, Westerly, Zaylia, Zemera. And thank you to Tara Carpenter and Christine van der Stege for their photograph contributions.

Thank you to my family and my friends for their encouragement and support. Thanks to Jenna for your insights and editing. Thank you to Jason for our initial collaboration; I am sad you will never see the fruition of that inspiration. Lastly, thank you to both my B's. Breah, you are my muse and the one I fight for the future for. Brad, you help me fly high and dive deep. I love you both.

Thank you to the wonderful editors and staff at Harbour Publishing for working with me on this project.

Acknowledgements

Selected References

Print

Dunbar-Ortiz, Roxanne. *An Indigenous Peoples' History of the United States for Young People*. Beacon Press, 2019.

Elpel, Thomas J. 1996. *Botany in a Day*. HOPS Press.

Kimmerer, Robin Wall. 2015. *Braiding Sweetgrass*. Milkweed Editions.

Sibley, David Allen. 2003. *The Sibley Field Guide to Birds of North America*. Alfred A. Knopf.

Young, Jon, Ellen Haas, and Evan McGown. 2010. *Coyote's Guide to Connecting with Nature*. OWLink.

Online

The Canadian Encyclopedia. "Indigenous Territory," by Molly Malone and Libby Chisholm. https://www.thecanadianencyclopedia.ca/en/article/indigenous-territory

Great Lakes Now. https://www.greatlakesnow.org/indigenous-voices-of-the-great-lakes/

Native Land Digital. http://native-land.ca/resources/territory-acknowledgement/

Ontario Trees and Shrubs. http://www.ontariotrees.com/

Ontario Wildflowers Field Guide. http://ontariowildflowers.com/

Index

Artists' Charcoal, 160

Aster, New England (*Symphyotrichum novae-angliae*), 151–52

Aster family (Asteraceae or Compositae), 19–20, 52, 107, 113, 126, 138, 153. *Also called* Sunflower family

Autumn Scavenger Hunt, 161

Basswood, American (*Tilia americana*), 37–38

Bear Hunt, Going on a, 75

Bee Balm (*Monarda fistulosa*), 98–100

Blackberry, 19, 34, 69, 128, 144

Blueberry, 10, 168–69

Bracken Fern (*Pteridium aquilinum*), 42–43

Buckthorn (*Rhamnus cathartica*), 30–32

Buckthorn Ink, Make Your Own, 31

Burdock, Common (*Arctium minus*), 107–108

Burdock Tag, Stealth, 108

Butterfly Garden, Grow a, 103

Carrot, Wild (*Daucus carota*), 2, 13, 22, 155–57. *Also called* Queen Anne's Lace

Carrot family (Apiaceae or Umbelliferae), 17–18, 22–23, 138

Cattail (*Typha latifolia*), 7, 44–47, 76

Cattail Ducks, 46

Cedar, 22, 124, 126–27

Eastern White Cedar (*Thuja occidentalis*), 170–71

Chickweed (*Stellaria media*), 48–50

Chokecherry (*Prunus virginiana*), 143

Coltsfoot (*Tussilago farfara*), 51

Cottonwood, 36

Eastern Cottonwood (*Populus deltoides*), 57–58. *Also called* Necklace Poplar

Cottonwood Bud Oil, Make Your Own, 59

Cougar Tracking, 181–82

Dandelion (*Taraxacum officinale*), 2, 50, 51, 52–56, 191

Dandelion Coffee, 54

Dandelion family, 20

Dogwood, Red Osier (*Cornus sericea*), 66

211

Early Wild Salad, 50

Elder
    Black Elder (*Sambucus canadensis*), 145
    Red Elder (*Sambucus racemosa* spp. *pubens*), 145

Elderberry Syrup, Make Your Own, 146–47

Fir, 10, 13, 63
    Balsam Fir (*Abies balsamea*), 163–64

Fireweed (*Epilobium angustifolium*), 111–12

Foxglove (*Digitalis purpurea*), 149

Garlic Mustard (*Alliaria petiolata*), 29–30

Ghost Pipe (*Monotropa uniflora*), 104–105

Giant Hogweed (*Heracleum mantegazzianum*), 23–25

Ginger, Wild (*Asarum canadense*), 89–91, 125

Goldenrod (*Solidago*), 148

Gosling Rescue Mission, 55–56

Grape, Wild (*Vitis vinifera* spp. *sylvestris*), 158–59

Guess this Bud, 186

Hawthorn (*Crataegus* spp.), 60

Healing Oil, Make Your Own, 122

Hemlock, Eastern (*Tsuga canadensis*), 167

herbalist, 3–4

Horsetail (*Equisetum arvense*), 63–64

Indigenous peoples
    colonization, 6–7
    digital map of traditional territories, 8
    Great Lakes region, of the, 6–7
    Plants, connection to, 6–8, 12–13

Japanese Knotweed (*Reynoutria japonica*), 32–34

Leek, Wild (*Allium tricoccum*), 93–94

Lily family (*Liliaceae*), 18

Magic Spells, 125

Magic Wands, 67

Maple
    Black Maple (*Acer nigrum*), 176
    Norway Maple (*Acer platanoides*), 176
    Sugar Maple (*Acer saccharum*), 176

Maple Syrup, Make Your Own, 177–78

Marsh Wander, 76

Measure a Fern, 43

Meet a Tree, 39

Memory Game, 65

Milkweed, Common (*Asclepias syriaca*), 101–102

Miner's Lettuce (*Claytonia perfoliate*), 48–50

Mint, Field (*Mentha arvensis*), 109–110

Mint family (*Mentha*), 18–19, 98

Missing Mint Mystery, The, 110

Mullein (*Verbascum thapsus*), 149–50

Nature Clock, 185

Nettle, Stinging (*Urtica dioica*), 80–82

Nettle-Spanakopita Grilled Cheese Sandwiches, 83

old-growth forest, 3, 168–69

One-Minute Mystery, 165

Oxeye Daisy (*Leucanthemum vulgare*), 113–14

Pine, Eastern White (*Pinus strobus*), 173–74

Pinecone Bird Feeders, 175

Plant Tag, 92

Plantain (Ribwort)
    Common Plantain (*Plantago major*), 115–19. *Also called* Oval Leaf Plantain
    English Plantain (*Plantago lanceolata*), 115–19. *Also called* Longleaf

Plantain Salve, Make Your Own, 117–19

Poison Hemlock (*Conium maculatum*), 17, 157
Poison Ivy (*Toxicodendron radicans*), 25–26
Poison Sumac (*Toxicodendron vernix*), 26–27
Pokeweed (*Phytolacca americana*), 27

Quiz, Tree, 189

Raccoon Tracking, 144
Raspberry, Wild (*Rubus idaeus*), 128
Raspberry Smoothie, 129
Red Oak (*Quercus rubra*), 183–84
Rose
    Prairie Rose (*Rosa setigera*), 68–69
    Prickly Wild Rose (*Rosa acicularis*), 68–69
    Swamp Rose (*Rosa palustris*), 68–69
Rose-petal Honey, Make Your Own, 70–72
Rose family (Rosaceae), 19, 60

school, nature, 3, 161
Sitting with Hawthorn, 61–62
Skunk Cabbage (*Symplocarpus foetidus*), 73–74
Spring Ephemeral Flowers, 88
Spring Scavenger Hunt, 96
Spruce (*Picea* spp.), 77–78
Spruce-tip Syrup, Make Your Own, 79

Strawberry
    Wild Strawberry (*Fragaria virginiana*), 130–32
    Woodland Strawberry (*Fragaria vesca*), 130–32
Summer Scavenger Hunt, 141
Sundew (*Drosera rotundifolia*), 123–24

Tansy (*Tanacetum vulgare*), 126–27
Tea
    Bee Balm Tea, Pick Your Own, 99
    Campfire Tea, 166
    Sun Tea, 110
Thistle
    Bull Thistle (*Cirsium vulgare*), 153–54
    Canada Thistle (*Cirsium arvense*), 153–54
Tinder, Make Your Own, 172
Trillium (*Trillium erectum*), 84–85
Trout Lily (*Erythronium americanum*), 86–87

Up Close and Personal activity, 106
Usnea (Old Man's Beard)
    Blood-Spattered Beard (*Usnea wirthii*), 179–80
    Methuselah's Beard (*Usnea longissima*), 179–80

Valentine's Day Card, 91
Violet, Blue (*Viola odorata*), 40
Violet Syrup, Make Your Own, 41

Viper's Bugloss (*Echium vulgare*), 136
Viper's Bugloss Ice Cubes, 137

Wall Kimmerer, Robin, 44–45
Water Hemlock (*Cicuta douglasii*), 21, 24, 157
    Spotted Water Hemlock (*Cicuta maculata*), 22–23
Who Am I? Game, 187
Wild Leek Pesto, 95
Wild Root Roast, 156–57
Willow
    Black Willow (*Salix nigra*), 133–34
    Sandbar Willow (*Salix exigua*), 133–34
    Shining Willow (*Salix lucida*), 133–34
Willow Crowns, 135
Winter Scavenger Hunt, 188
Wort, St. John's (*Hypericum perforatum*), 120–21

Yarrow (*Achillea millefolium*), 138
Yarrow First Aid, 139–40

Image Credits

Adobe Stock

p.i: Cavan / p.vii: Chase D'Animulls / p.viii: Sandra Standbridge / p.20 top: far700 / p.22: Inga / p.23: Inga / p.24: Georgy Dzyura / p.25: Lost_in_the_Midwest / p.26: Ruckszio / p.27: dvulikaia / p.29: wiha3 / p.31 top: Oleh Marchak / p.31 bottom: Kateryna / p.33: Tomas Vynikal / p.38: Jurga Jot / p.41: vermontalm / p.49 top: Stefan / p.49 bottom: LifeisticAC / p.56: davidhoffmann.com / p.51: Iwona / p.62: Lyubov / p.64: Oleh Marchak / p.66 bottom: Denny / p.74 bottom: Denny / p.77 bottom: Lev Paraskevopoulos / p.83: Walid / p.84: Kristina Blokhin / p.86 bottom: mbruxelle / p.88: Donna Bollenbach / p.93: Sarawut / p.94 top: Brent Hofacker / p.94 bottom: FotoHelin / p.95: Anton / p.100: Dan Barron / p.102: yvonne navalaney / p.103: Margaret Burlingham / p.112 right: Shaye / p.121: Rhönbergfoto / p.122: Madeleine Steinbach / p.125: Nola V/ peopleimages.com / p.126: Karin Jähne / p.129: pawle / p.137: bennytrapp / p.143 bottom: Danicha / p.147: Norkaph / p.159: Lovin' it on Phuket / p.162: MNStudio / p.171 bottom: Anna / p.174: Lori Swadley / p.182: Danita Delimont / p.184 left: andybirkey / p.184 right: redtbird02 / p.185: H_Ko

Katrina Rain Photography

p.43 / p.50 / p.54 top and bottom / p.59 / p.71 left and right / p.72 / p.81 / p.91 / p.117 / p.118 / p.119 / p.135 / p.139 / p.150 / p.172 bottom / p.177 / p.186 / p.194 / p.195 / p.196 / p.199 / p.201

Christine van der Stege

p.ii / p.10 / p.11 / p.78 top and bottom / p.79 all photos / p.112 left / p.142 / p.161 top and bottom / p.164 / p.190 / p.192

Tara Carpenter

p.5 / p.8 / p.15 / p.165

Ariel Brewster

p.171 top / p.188 / p.189

Stocksy

p.97: 102766, Brian Powell

All others by the author.

About the Author

Philippa Joly is a clinical community herbalist, paramedic and outdoor educator. She runs an outdoor school for kids and leads workshops on herbal medicine, plant identification, ethical wildcrafting, herbal first aid, local healing plants and anticolonial approaches to wellness. She lives on Denman Island, BC, with her plant-savvy daughter, Breah, and their dog, Theodore Fox, and grey cat, Casey. If you want to find out more or write Philippa a letter, visit her website: philippajoly.com

Copyright © 2025 Philippa Joly

1 2 3 4 5 — 29 28 27 26 25

All rights reserved. No part of this publication may be reproduced, stored in a retrieval system or transmitted, in any form or by any means, without prior permission of the publisher or, in the case of photocopying or other reprographic copying, a licence from Access Copyright, www.accesscopyright.ca, 1-800-893-5777, info@accesscopyright.ca.

Harbour Publishing Co. Ltd.
P.O. Box 219, Madeira Park, BC, V0N 2H0
www.harbourpublishing.com

Edited by Rachel Heinrichs
Indexed by Colleen Bidner
Cover and text design by Libris Simas Ferraz / Onça Publishing
Cover photography: Top middle: Adobe Stock by rabbitti; Top right: Katrina Rain Photography; Bottom middle: Adobe Stock by Eva. All others by the author.
Printed and bound in South Korea
Printed with vegetable-based ink on paper certified by the Forest Stewardship Council®

Harbour Publishing acknowledges the support of the Canada Council for the Arts, the Government of Canada, and the Province of British Columbia through the BC Arts Council.

Library and Archives Canada
Cataloguing in Publication

Title: A kid's guide to plants of the Great Lakes region : including Southern Ontario, with cool facts, activities and recipes / Philippa Joly.
Other titles: Plants of the Great Lakes region
Names: Joly, Philippa, author.
Description: Includes bibliographical references and index.
Identifiers: Canadiana (print) 20240524853 | Canadiana (ebook) 20240524861 | ISBN 9781998526109 (softcover) | ISBN 9781998526116 (EPUB)
Subjects: LCSH: Plants—Great Lakes Region (North America)—Identification—Juvenile literature. | LCSH: Plants—Great Lakes Region (North America)—Juvenile literature. | LCSH: Botany—Great Lakes Region (North America)—Juvenile literature. | LCGFT: Field guides. | LCGFT: Activity books.
Classification: LCC QK130 .J65 2025 | DDC j581.977—dc23